HOW TO MAKE HOT COLD CALLS

THIRD EDITION
REVISED AND UPDATED

STEVEN J. SCHWARTZ

Fitzhenry & Whiteside

How to Make Hot Cold Calls, Third Edition
Copyright © 2006, 2001, 1997 by Steven J. Schwartz

All inquiries should be addressed to:

Fitzhenry and Whiteside Limited
195 Allstate Parkway
Markham, Ontario L3R 4T8

In the United States:
311 Washington Street
Brighton, Massachusetts 02135

www.fitzhenry.ca   godwit@fitzhenry.ca

Fitzhenry & Whiteside acknowledges with thanks the Canada Council
for the Arts, and the Ontario Arts Council for their support of our
publishing program. We acknowledge the financial support of the
Government of Canada through the Book Publishing Industry
Development Program (BPIDP) for our publishing activities.

Library and Archives Canada Cataloguing in Publication

Schwartz, Steven J., 1956–
How to make hot cold calls / Steven J. Schwartz.
3rd ed., rev. and updated

ISBN 1-55005-133-4

1. Telephone selling.   I. Title.

HF5438.3.S38   2005   658.8'72   C2005-903508-0

United States Cataloging-in-Publication Data

Schwartz, Steven J., 1956–
How to make hot cold calls / Steven J. Schwartz.
3rd ed.
[200] p. : ill. ; cm.

Summary: A how to guide for anyone in the business,
sales or telemarketing world, wanting to improve their sales
or land the perfect job.

ISBN 1-55005-133-4 (pbk.)

1. Telephone selling. 2. Telemarketing. I. Title.

658.85 dc22   HF5438.3.S38

Design and typesetting: Kinetics Design & Illustration
Cover design, based on original design by Angel Guerra.
Illustrations: Bill Slavin at Kinder Box
Call Caffeine® is a registered trademark of SJS Productions Inc.

Printed and bound in Canada

1 3 5 7 9 10 8 6 4 2

In memory of

my mother
who always told me to pick up the telephone and call

and my little brother Michael
who made some great calls of his own

Contents

Preface to the Third Edition

You would think that after publishing a best-selling revised edition of *How To Make Hot Cold Calls* I would leave well enough alone. I'm a Virgo, which means I'm a perfectionist, and so if there are new ideas evolving from my system that will give my readers even greater value, I'm going to invest the time and get those gems into your hands.

This third edition is still very much a "how to" kind of book designed for helping you achieve results. If you already own a copy of my previous editions you will profit equally from the enhancements in this latest edition. You'll discover dozens of additional techniques and tips; these are not just enhancements but also priceless insights from readers who took this system to heights I hadn't imagined. I also took it upon myself to do a major revamp of the scripting section because I felt that my audience was now ready to take this system to the next level. The scripting material is now more focused on the power of developing imagery, plus there is more insight on how to sell into vertical markets.

With so many people enjoying the success of getting in the door with *Hot Cold Calls*, I recently published the sequel, *So Your Foot's In The Door... Now What?* This sequel builds on the very skills and behaviors that the *Hot Cold Calls* system gives you, and takes the guesswork out of face-to-face sales calls. Once you make the initial customer connection through *Hot Cold Calls*, *Foot's In The Door* will show you how to stay connected until the sale is made. If you are already applying the methods from *Foot's In The Door*, you will find many of the concepts in this book familiar. And if you have not read the sequel by now, what are you waiting for?

It's time to settle in and learn something that will change your life.

I look forward to hearing your success stories.

STEVEN J. SCHWARTZ

Introduction

"Hello!"

That's either the complete vocabulary of a cheap parrot, or the first step in the business of making successful telephone sales calls. As I have considerable experience with the latter, and have never even owned a budgie, let's talk about how I'm going to get you to book more sales appointments over the telephone than you ever dreamed possible. We're talking, of course, about mastering the infamous "Cold Call."

Hey! What did I say? Don't run away . . .

Funny how two simple words strike fear into the hearts and minds of millions. When the police chase a criminal down the street and holler, "Freeze!" they might as well shout, "Make a Cold Call!" I mean, who do you know who actually likes the idea — let alone the reality — of picking up the telephone to call a stranger, with the intent of making that unknown entity feel compelled to see them. Anyone?

I promise not to use the "C" word again if you promise not to run away. Deal? I'll just refer to the term "telephone sales calls" instead. Making telephone sales calls is the art of using the telephone to introduce yourself and your products and services, with the intent of either selling directly over the telephone or setting up sales appointments. Think of the telephone sales call as nothing more than your calling card. *You can't sell your service or product if you can't get in the door.* This is true for salespeople of course. But it is equally true for the self-employed, who have to spend just as much time at sales as salespeople. And if you're unemployed and calling on companies for work, the product you're selling is you.

"I'm not in business."

People apply this system in all parts of their personal lives, because everyone has to reach and influence decision makers at one point or another. For example:

- You might be in a neighborhood or school committee where you have to get some idea or reform off the ground.
- You might want to go back to school and need a way to get your application noticed and approved.
- You may have a teenager who needs to apply for his or her first job.
- What about all those times when you have a complaint about bad service and want a company to make things right?

- Let's not forget about that dream you want to build; you'll need the support of others to make it happen.

"I'm in sales."

If you're in sales, gone are the days when you could own the best product and have customers banging down your door to get it — even if you were selling a digitized mousetrap. These days you have to go out there and drag in the business. Customers aren't going to come to you — you have to go to them. Oh, did I mention the competition yet? Nasty business. It's everywhere. Unrelenting. Merciless. And very hungry. (Your competition has probably already devoured this book!) They are calling on prospective customers as we speak, especially on *your* customers. For you, my friends, telephone sales calls are the life-blood of your business, which is all the more reason why you need to get good and comfortable with the idea of making those calls. When you reach the point, with the help of this book, where making telephone sales calls is as natural as brushing your teeth, your sales and job satisfaction are going to shine.

"I'm not in sales. I'm self-employed."

If you're self-employed (an entrepreneur, consultant) you ought to know that you are in fact in sales. No one knows you're there if you don't reach out and tell them. Unless your clients are running to you in great hordes not seen since the likes of Genghis Khan, you have to go out there and get 'em. Learning how to make successful telephone sales calls gives you the power to take control of your sales and increase revenues.

"I'm looking for venture capital."

If you're an entrepreneur in search of funding, your elevator pitch has only seconds to catch the attention of would-be lenders. The ability to reach venture capitalists and deliver a compelling vision of your idea is an important prerequisite for success.

"I don't make many calls."

The fewer calls you make, the less room you have to make mistakes. This system is all about precision, not volume. With so much riding on one call, you have to take the guesswork out of the outcome. It's also a good idea to take this opportunity to widen your circle of influence.

"I don't need to worry because I work on referrals."

Referrals do not guarantee appointments. A referral is like having an ace in a poker hand. It gives you an edge, but winning comes down to how you play that card. Another point worth noting: In order to keep your referrals coming, you need to ensure that you make a positive professional engagement so the person who referred you looks good. And since your first call is the beginning of the customer relationship, the impression you make, and the expectations you set in motion, have to be perfect so the rest of your sales cycle will be shorter.

"I'm looking for employment."

Let's not forget the soon-to-be-employed. One sure way to move out of your unemployed status is to use the telephone effectively to follow up your carefully crafted résumé and get yourself an interview. With so many other people ahead of you in line asking for appointments, one successful call from you can put you ahead of the pack and on the road to a brighter future. And if you don't know to whom you should send your polished résumé, the telephone is your fast track to networking, the art of speaking to as many people as possible to uncover opportunities and spread your name around.

No matter where you're coming from, a good part of your current apprehension about making telephone sales calls comes from the discomfort of not knowing what to do, what to say, how to say it, how to think, how to plan, etc. By buying this book you've already taken the first positive step to increasing your knowledge. I might add, this is more than just a book. It's a *systematic approach* to making telephone sales calls that will boost your confidence and, consequently, fill up your appointment book. The operative word here is "systematic."

A system gives you two things you need to reach any goal: Consistency and predictability. You can't have predictability without consistency, and you can't have consistency without a system. A system is a series of well-defined steps that work in concert to achieve success. Instead of taking a hit-and-miss approach to sales calls, I'd like to give you the security of an approach that works time in and time out. In other words, it's time to take the guesswork out of calling and learn a system that is proven to make your calls successful.

This highly original system takes an entirely fresh approach to telephone sales calls. I'm going to show you new, innovative techniques to help you:

- Overcome your fear of sales calls with effective strategies for turning your negative fears into positive feelings
- Reach every person you want to, and in the shortest period of time, by putting you in control of the entire call process
- Develop a more effective way of creating a telephone sales script by creating a strategically defined sales pitch
- Leverage the power of words and the images they create
- Deliver your message with confidence and persuasion by applying my innovative delivery techniques

- Condition yourself to be motivated at a moment's notice with Call Caffeine®, a series of fourteen stimulating techniques to keep you energized and focused
- Identify problems and resolve them quickly

In the process, I'll even show you how to *enjoy* making sales calls! (If you're not with me on that last one, you will be by the time we finish.) This book is a lot of fun. It's very interactive, with all kinds of thought-provoking workshops for you to participate in. In fact, the exercises are an integral part of the learning process. So the more you participate, the more successful you'll be.

Time to put on your shades.

You're about to see something new under the sun.

1

The Telephone Commercial

*B*efore I offer you my advice on anything, I feel I must earn your trust. I'm sure you will more readily take the advice of someone who has been in your shoes. Walked your walk. Talked your talk. Let me assure you, I've been where you are today. When it comes to being afraid of picking up the telephone to make sales calls, not knowing what to do, and hating every moment of it, I've been there, done that, and bought the T-shirt.

How to Make Hot Cold Calls was inspired by the Mother of Invention on a particularly ordinary day twenty-five years ago, when I first started my own business. I remember the day well. In fact, I'll never forget it. Come with me to that fateful beginning in 1980 . . .

I had just begun my career as an advertising copywriter and the world was my oyster. I loved what I did, and thought my employment would go on forever. Why shouldn't it? At twenty-four years old, I was a mere puppy. A Jimmy Olsen. Hey, life was a slice.

Slice. Slice. Slice.

Unfortunately, that was the sound of budgets being cut. Since advertising agencies embrace last-in-first-out-based slicing, your humble scribe here got the axe and a complimentary introduction to the world of unemployment. That was accompanied by enrollment in the school of hard knocks, from which I am proud to say I have since graduated with honors. I approached many advertising agencies, but it being September, agencies were in budget mode, not hiring mode. I figured if no one was going to hire me, I would hire myself, and overnight became a self-employed advertising copywriter. Through a series of fortuitous referrals, things went great for the first year. And then the recession of '81 rolled in like a thick morning fog on Vancouver Island.

I learned quickly that no one was going to beat a path to my door. I had to open the doors myself. No shortcuts here. I had to call up companies and sell my services, or at least sell the *idea* that my service was important enough for them to discuss it further with me in person. As a result, I started making telephone sales calls. Lots of them.

I have news for you. In one respect I was no different from you; I was scared to death of sales calls. (The only other time I was that scared was when I was six years old watching Boris Karloff come down that long, forbidding staircase.) It took me hours to get my nerve up to make those calls. Hours. My success? Truthfully, if I made ten calls I would be lucky to get one appointment — "lucky" being the operative word. I felt a knot in the pit of my stomach every time I made a call. I wasn't concerned about selling someone on my abilities once I saw them in person, but call them on the telephone? Forget it! And the business of trying to get a hold of anyone? That was a whole other experience.

Then one day I had had enough.

I mean, I was royally fed up with the rejection, fed up with the frustration, and just plain fed up with my stomach churning like a gristmill on a cold day. (Any of this sound familiar?) Taking comfort in my belief that obstacles are merely creative challenges, I knew there had to be a better way to do this — and I was going to find it! One day I decided to analyze the situation, in true Virgo fashion. I instinctively knew that there had to be a system for doing it "the right way." A system would allow me to do it right all the time, which would boost my confidence and send those butterflies in my stomach off to winter migration. But what kind of system? Hmmmm . . . figuring that out meant coming to terms with questions like, What the heck is a telephone sales call anyway? I pondered a series of logical questions and answers . . .

Q: *What is the process of making unsolicited telephone sales calls?*

A: *There is a series of actions I have to take. First I have to know who I want to call, then I have to get a hold of that person — which means knowing where to reach them, and then being motivated to pick up the telephone to call — and then I have to convince them to see me — which means I have to know what to say, and how to say it convincingly.*

Q: *What am I actually doing when I'm making a telephone sales call?*

A: *I'm calling people on the telephone.*

Q: *Why?*

A: *To deliver a sales message.*

Q: *What message am I sending?*

A: *I'm advertising the things that make my service unique.*

Q: *How do I create this advertisement?*

A: *As for any advertisement; the message has to be tailored to the specific medium I'm using.*

Q: *What medium am I using?*

A: *It's not a print medium, because my message is not communicated through magazines, newspapers, or brochures. It obviously isn't television. The telephone is an electronic medium, though. That leaves radio. Wait a minute! Radio! That's it! My audience isn't reading my message or watching it, they're listening to it. Like a radio commercial, my message is delivered through the airwaves without visual communication. And like radio, it is heard over a speaker — the telephone receiver. So that's it. The telephone sales call is an advertised message delivered much like a radio commercial. However, since I'm using a telephone and not the radio, my sales message is not a radio commercial but rather a telephone commercial.*

Q: *What is a "telephone commercial"?*

A: *Since a telephone sales call is like a radio commercial,*
   - *You have less than thirty seconds to get your message through*
   - *You have to earn every second of your listener's time*
   - *You can't see your audience, so what you say and how you say it will be critical*
   - *The patter must be scripted like any other commercial message: strategically defined, with each word carefully chosen to keep your audience listening*
   - *To compensate for the fact that your message is being*

carried over thousands of miles of wire, your delivery (how you talk) has to be highly energetic and enthusiastic

- *You will have to know the best time of day/week/month to reach your intended audience*

My answers changed everything. At last, instead of working in the dark, I had a formula for creating my telephone sales pitch. I immediately took to the task of putting together my own telephone commercial. For the next two days I strategically defined what I wanted to say, and then took another day to rehearse how I was going to say it. (I had previous experience acting in many radio commercials.) Then it was time to test my commercial. I drew up a list of twenty people to call, and then went for broke.

The results showed me that I was on to something that was more than just coincidence. Out of twenty calls, I got eighteen appointments. A fluke? No way! Not with that kind of success. Most important, I discovered that I now had an approach I could duplicate to do well consistently. More confident than ever, I made another series of calls — a *call campaign* — and achieved the same results.

I had a system. And I've never looked back.

With a system that I could count on time in and time out for making successful telephone sales calls, my confidence increased to the point where I started *enjoying* making the calls, because I knew with one hundred percent certainty that those calls were leading to appointments, which were making my business successful. I still love making those calls today because, quite frankly, they're still growing my business. In fact, my telephone commercial system became a second business altogether, as I was asked by my corporate clients to duplicate my success and help them increase the effectiveness of their telemarketing programs.

Now it's time to make *your* business more successful.

2

Overcoming
Fear

Fear of making telephone sales calls is as old as
. . . well . . . old as sales itself. Why, even before the telephone was invented, I'm sure there were all kinds of people
who were apprehensive about making sales calls. I take you
back now to ancient Greece — Athens in the fifth century
B.C. — where two traders are standing at the gates of this
prosperous city-state talking about their displeasure over
making sales calls. (If you think calling for appointments

over the telephone is uncomfortable, how would you like to be one of our two trusty traders, *sans* telephones, tying messages around the legs of carrier pigeons?)

Hector: I have many bottles of wine to ship to Crete. I have only to find as many buyers.

Orestes: (*Tearing up paper into little pieces.*) And I have fishing nets enough to shower the vessels of Thebes. But the fishermen ask so many questions, I must be prepared with all the answers.

Hector: Why are you tearing up your message before securing it to the foot of your messenger?

Orestes: Alas, my message is too long, and I fear that unless I shorten what I have to say, the consequences will be dire.

Hector: You are afraid your prospects will not listen to such a long message?

Orestes: Yes. But more important, I am afraid the messenger will not be able to fly with such a weighty response.

Hector: At least you send a message of good offerings. I cannot.

Orestes: And why is that? Have you no messengers to carry your words?

Hector: Yes, but that is not it. I am afraid to do such a thing as that. And when I am afraid, I get depressed. And when I get depressed, I eat.

Orestes: But how can your eating affect your work?

Hector: I get so depressed I eat the damned birds. And then none of my sales get off the ground.

Orestes: The Fates have sealed your destiny.

Hector: No, it is I who seal my destiny. I cannot stomach the thought of sending messages as you do.

Orestes: Surely you stomach plenty.

Hector: You are too kind, dear friend. But tell me, by what force do you persevere?

Orestes: Ahh, I wing it.

Times haven't changed much. Almost everyone I speak to today has a horror story about making telephone sales calls, because most people are either simply uncomfortable and apprehensive about making those calls, or are completely gripped by fear. Do you fall within that range? Fear paralyses you, putting on hold not just the telephone, but all your dreams and aspirations. Don't believe me? Then think about this:

If you don't pick up the telephone, absolutely nothing is going to happen. No telephone sales calls. No appointments. No sales. No work. No chance of realizing your dreams. However, by making the calls, you create the leads, appointments, sales, and employment; this moves you closer to realizing your goals, dreams, and aspirations. That's why the first step to making successful telephone sales calls is having the ability to actually pick up the telephone.

I want you to know that I've been there too. I had a Ph.D. in procrastination. But I overcame my fear, or should I say, I *learned* how to overcome my fear. You can too. As I mentioned earlier, when I was starting out in my own business I was terrified, and not just about what I was going to say to a total stranger. Just getting up the nerve to pick up the telephone was overwhelming. It was upsetting enough to think about making one sales call; you should have seen my reaction to the thought of making a second, third, or fourth call. That was pushing it! Now don't get me wrong, I'm a highly motivated individual, by nature. But this was a fear in a league of its own.

I remember when I was a kid I had a fear of deep water, and nothing, absolutely nothing could get me to jump into the deep end of the swimming pool. You couldn't even get me to walk around the deep end. Well, when it came to sales calls, the telephone seemed like a diving board over the deepest, coldest part of that pool. I just couldn't make myself take the big leap. Hardly surprising. I was afraid.

Most people will not do things they are afraid of. I don't. Do you? If you're afraid of heights (as I am) you wouldn't climb up a ladder. If you're afraid of airplanes, you'd take the train. If you're afraid of making telephone sales calls . . . Exactly. Well then, logic dictates the following remedy: *Take away the fear, and the sales calls will follow.*

Easier said than done? Like I said, I've been there, and while it wasn't easy to erase my fear, it was possible, and it happened. *I changed my negative reaction to making telephone sales calls by building the skills that would overcome the way I felt.* You're about to learn the same skills, beginning with how to acknowledge your fear; once you know where your fear is coming from, you can turn it into something positive. Let's get started.

Acknowledge and Embrace Your Fear/Apprehension

It's one thing to know that you don't want to pick up the telephone, and it's quite another to acknowledge your fear or apprehension. In the beginning, I knew that I was afraid of making the calls, but rather than acknowledge and confront my fear, I ran away from it — and from the telephone too. I invented countless excuses why I shouldn't reach for the telephone. Sound familiar? I had so many excuses, in fact, that I could fill a book with them. (There's a whole litany of them in the introduction to the Call Caffeine section. You're sure to recognize many of your own "famous excuses" among them.) Do yourself a favor and put your excuses aside for now. Face the fact that the last thing you ever want to do is pick up the telephone to make sales calls. That's OK. You're not alone. Your apprehension is not only perfectly understandable, it's normal. Embrace your apprehension for a minute. Remember it's *your* fear, which makes it very personal. Your fear is as individual to you as your thumbprint, with one exception: You can wipe your hands of fear.

Now remember in the introduction I mentioned that this is a very interactive book, with lots of workshops for you to take part in. While the exercises are interesting and fun, they are specially designed to help you learn, and to apply the knowledge you're gaining. Your first series of exercises helps you take ownership of your fear and apprehension. I trust you will make every effort to participate.

Drawing is an effective learning technique, one I use often. It's not the quality of your drawing that's important, it's the act of drawing that facilitates learning. Take out your markers, or better yet bum a few crayons off your children.

Render how it feels to make telephone sales calls. (Take all the time you need.)

See that picture? That's your own fear you have illustrated. Now that you know what your fear looks like, you have the ability to erase it from your mind.

Think of the last few times that you made telephone sales calls. What were you feeling when you made those calls, and where were you feeling it?

Describe your behavior when you made those telephone sales calls.

_____

_____

Why was it hard to make those calls?

_____

_____

What were you saying to yourself as you made the calls?

_____

_____

At this point you clearly know what your fear looks like, and the powerful, negative effect it has on you — physically and mentally. It's a very real thing, isn't it? You can see it. You can feel it. Take that very real picture you have of your fear, and your expression of how it affects you, and ask yourself the following question:

If you were not afraid to make telephone sales calls, what would you be, and how would you be different?

_____

_____

Now illustrate your answer.

Now you have a clear impression of what it's like *not being afraid* of making telephone sales calls. A few minutes ago you barely acknowledged your fear and, as result, you had in mind no clear alternative to that fear. *You now have a positive vision of what is possible.* Don't ever underestimate the power of that vision. Every person is a visual being, in that we all move in the direction of our visions. Suppose I were to say to you, "You know that hole in the front yard? You're always falling into it, so don't slip and fall into the hole in the front yard." What image comes to mind? Do you see yourself falling into the hole in the front yard? Because your focus is on falling into the hole, you'll probably fall into the hole. On the other hand, what if I were to say to you, "You know that hole in the front yard? Could you make sure that you walk around it next time?" Since your focus is on walking around the hole, that's exactly what you will do.

That's the power of visualization.

(This is a true story: Just this afternoon, I dropped by to say hello to a neighbor across the street. She was telling her daughter not to frown, and sure enough all her daughter could do was frown. I turned to her adorable four-year-old and said, "Don't smile!" You got it. She smiled.)

Since you and I react to mental images, we will live happier lives if we keep our visions positive. Go back to the drawings you did a little while ago. If you keep your focus on your first drawing, that's where you'll stay. You painted a negative picture, and because that was all your mind focused on, you moved in the direction of that image. You saw fear and apprehension, and you then felt fear and apprehension. That's about to change.

With the second drawing you replaced your negative vision with a new, positive image that is every bit as real. It is an inspiring vision of what it would be like if you were not afraid of making telephone sales calls.

Stay focused on that positive vision of yourself, and that's how you will end up.

When you believe that your outcome will be more positive, your expectations are greater. This in turn makes your attitude more positive, which translates into action: picking up the telephone and making those all-important calls.

Just as surely as your first vision inspired fear and, in the process, gave rise to destructive habits (procrastination, avoidance), the new, positive image you have just created will give birth to new, winning habits (making telephone sales calls, envisioning success) that give you a direction and something to hold on to. With that new, positive image in mind, let's take the next step towards realizing that vision.

Analyze Your Fear

Fear is a negative force. My friends who are more scientifically inclined tell me that anything negative cannot at the same time be positive. You and I are focusing on the positive, right? Think about what would happen if we turned the negative (–) into something positive (+). Your fear would be gone. Grounded. But just what kind of fear are we talking about? Lurking in the depths of your mind lie the four Cardinal Fears: fear of the unknown, fear of technology, fear of rejection, and fear of failure.

Let's take these negatives, examine where they come from and what they mean, and then turn them into something positive and constructive.

Fear of the Unknown

Let's go on a trip. You drive. Better fill up with gas, we're going to need it. All set? Oh, you want to know where we're going? Far away. Thousands of miles away, to a place you've never travelled before. I forgot to mention that we don't have a map and we're leaving at night, in the pouring rain. Comfortable? Ready to go? No? I don't blame you. Nobody wants to go off without knowing where they're going or how to get there. Journeying directionless into uncharted territory in bad conditions sounds like making sales calls, doesn't it?

Part of your overall uneasiness is that you are making telephone sales calls in the dark. The sales call is a complex process, and on the road to making successful sales calls there are all kinds of details to familiarize yourself with. If you do not have the experience to negotiate the various twists and turns, it's only natural that you'll be apprehensive about making these calls. I can teach you to eliminate your fear of the unknown by shedding light on your dark road, finding the right direction, and arriving at your destination. Like any map worth its salt, the more you study my techniques, the easier it will be to get to your destination. So I'll tell you what. You read on. Leave the navigating to me, for now.

Fear of Technology

When was the last time you enjoyed connecting a new stereo or DVD? (Does your old VCR still flash 12:00, even though it's 3:45?) How long did it take you to get your computer up and running? Once you did, did you enjoy using it? Right away?

If you're like most people, you don't easily warm up to technology. While it has no doubt improved our lives, technical equipment can seem foreign to our way of thinking. "Techies" design the machinery and write the manuals, and we regular mortals are left in awe that the the equipment runs at all. And when the machinery breaks down, good luck fixing it. I'm no Einstein, are you? No wonder technology is often perceived as being cold and impersonal. After all, we are not machines.

The telephone is a technological wonder that is no

different than any other piece of electronic equipment. Technology works in ways we don't understand, enforcing a "cooler" image, which is hard to warm up to. Cold is not motivating. Warm is. That being the case, what is it about telephones that lends itself quite naturally to preying on your fears? You know me by now. I'm not going to spill the beans *that* fast! Try this exercise first:

Look around the room and pick any object you see. Whatever it happens to be, that's what I'd like you to sell me. Well, come on. I'm a willing customer. Sell it to me. What's the matter? What do you mean you can't sell me that item? Why not? Oh, you're not comfortable with the fact that you can't communicate with me face to face? Funny. That's the same problem with using the telephone.

Telephones just don't allow us to communicate in a natural manner; we are forced to talk to each other electronically over miles of wires, as opposed to personally, face to face. (That may all change one day when the video telephone is in every home.) Normally this is not a problem, because we've been socialized to enjoy talking to people on the telephone. It only becomes a problem when the telephone call you are making happens to be a sales call; then the whole dynamic of the situation changes dramatically. Suddenly communicating with a total stranger is a scarier prospect. Not knowing what people look like or how they're reacting to you is extremely unsettling.

Remember that item you wanted to sell me? If you had your choice, would you prefer to meet over the telephone or in person? Thought so. Let's face it, there's no substitute for a face-to-face meeting. Any salesperson would rather sell to a prospective customer in person than over the telephone (even though it's not as cost-effective). Why do you suppose that is? Well, for one thing, initial impressions speak volumes and, unfortunately, eighty percent of the impression you make comes from your body language, which, as you know, is not on your side when it comes to using the telephone. Another reason might be that you can size someone up a lot more quickly when you see that individual. You can tell if they're interested, and react accordingly if they're not. You can *feel* if there's any chemistry between you.

That body language I spoke of allows you to communicate more aggressively; you can lean in closer to the person, look into their eyes, talk with your hands. If you're tall you can command instant respect, and if you're attractive, you already have their attention. Is any of that possible over the telephone? Hardly. What happens when you're not feeling well, you have an off day, and you're just not "you" today? If you are selling to me in person you could disguise the way you feel by hiding behind your body language, or if you're nervous, you can warm up with some small talk. I would never know that you were uncomfortable.

But try that over the telephone! No, sorry, no can do. No body language here. No small talk either. No handshake. No smile. No physical connection whatsoever. Not even a warm welcome. (At least when you see someone in person you arrange an appointment. With a sales call you come unannounced, often at an inopportune moment.) What's worse, if you were calling me I could sense any apprehension or insincerity in seconds flat. "Hello" is as far as you'd need to go before you were pegged. Add it all up, and is it any wonder you're afraid to place a sales call to someone you don't know? The whole procedure can be unnatural, uncomfortable, and unnerving. The lack of body language creates a barrier between you and the person you are calling, making the call feel impersonal and "cold." But take heart. All is not lost. Here's a secret.

All you have to do is transform an impersonal call into a personal call.

Turning a call to a stranger you can't see into a conversation with a personal friend makes an impersonal call a warm encounter. The strategy is to familiarize yourself with the person you are about to call. For example, right now if I were calling you, I wouldn't know what you looked like or sounded like, or anything else about you for that matter. The more I knew about you, the more familiar with you I would become, and the less important my reliance on body language would be. You do this all the time when you talk with your friends and acquaintances. If you and I had already met, we wouldn't feel uncomfortable talking to each other without seeing our body language, would we? Stay tuned. You'll have the opportunity to learn several effective techniques for familiarizing yourself with your prospects, in the upcoming sections. (In the Call Planning chapter see Voicefinder; in the Call Caffeine chapter see Double Cream All Sugar, Friends, and All Clear.)

Creating a personalized call is only half the picture here. A second strategy for overcoming a fear of technology is to use the telephone like any other piece of office equipment. Take your computer as an example. Like any computer, a telephone is not comfortable to work with at first. But ask yourself, if your computer was so difficult to work with at first, why did you continue to work with it, and what effect did the continued use have on you? The more you used the computer, the more valuable you saw it to be. Therefore, you continued to use it. The cycle continued: greater use led to greater appreciation, which led to greater use, and so on.

The more you use the telephone, the more you will appreciate how effective it is in helping you to achieve your goals.

The more goals you realize (making money, creating opportunities, finding employment, making dreams come true), the more you will use the telephone in striving to achieve your goals. In the end, the telephone is no different than your computer, DVD, or any other piece of technology you use to improve your life, which is what I've said all along.

Easier said than done, you say. Granted, before you could use your computer on an ongoing basis, you had to first get over the hurdle of using it at all. There were a few steps you had to take between the time you first took your computer out of the box (and passed out from shock at the size of the manual) and the time you gathered enough confidence to use it often. I'd like you to think back to something that was difficult or overwhelming for you to do at the beginning, but which is now second nature, such as working a computer, programming your DVD or fax machine.

Write down and prioritize the process you went through to get over the first few hurdles of using technology.

_____
_____
_____

How can you repeat that process with your telephone sales calls?

_____
_____
_____

From my own experience, I can recall the first time I got my new fax machine. It came with a big booklet full of whiz-bang features. I didn't look at a single one. I was terrified. So what did I do? I did what I always do in a situation like that. I took the machine out of the wrapping and plugged it in. Then I took a break. Then I looked for the basic features, like setting my name, the time, and the date. I did that one feature at a time. And I took my dear sweet time. If I got stuck, I called a friend. Or two. Or three. But I got started with the basics.

Slowly, over time, the more I used the fax machine, the more I experienced the power of that technology to communicate in a timely and cost-efficient manner. I began to use new features, one at time. I was willing to overlook the discomfort of learning all the features because I saw the value in using the fax machine for communication. Consequently, I kept on faxing. The more fax calls I made, the more confident I felt learning new features, which only further enhanced the value of the product.

In the same way, calling complete strangers is also awkward at first, but once you start booking appointments you will begin to see the value in using the telephone to drum up business. That initial success will encourage you to continue. The more you make successful telephone sales calls the more natural the process will become. The telephone might start out as an obstacle, but it ends up as an asset. It's indispensable. Invaluable. And it will allow you to pull in a better income.

Although a fear of technology can make the telephone look like a barrier between you and your prospects, the value in using the telephone to make sales calls is that it actually brings you and prospective customers together.

Fear of Rejection

What's the number-one thing anyone will tell you when you talk about the fear of rejection?

Survey says: You can't take rejection personally.

Those words, nice as they are, don't cut it. Since you've heard that line a million times before, if it *really* worked — if all it took to rid yourself of your fear of rejection was some well intentioned person uttering the magic words, *You can't take rejection personally* — you'd already have run past this section faster than a chicken in barbecue season, because you would have no fear of rejection by now.

When I started putting this system together all those years ago, this was the first fear I analyzed and defeated. Quickly. This has to be the number-one fear that holds everyone back from making telephone sales calls. To be honest, it's a bit of a mystery to me. I've often wondered why people feel rejected when they are turned down by someone they've never met. If you were a street vendor and a total stranger came up to you, listened to your sales pitch, and then said, "No thanks. I'm not interested," would you be devastated? Would you take it personally? If you did, you wouldn't be in business for very long. Telephone sales calls are no different. Why take it personally when someone turns you down over the telephone? This is business.

You're simply doing your job. So do it professionally. That begins with understanding that every sales call is not going to be a success, especially at the beginning when you're just learning how to make successful telephone sales calls. No matter how good you are at selling, you will always have a few calls that don't pan out for whatever reason. It goes with the territory. All you need to do is plan in advance for how to deal with this reality.

So let's talk strategy. Here are four proven strategies I'd like to share with you:

1. Anticipate rejection
2. Change your thinking
3. Reduce the possibility of being turned down
4. Stay focused on success

1. Anticipate rejection
Whenever people try to cope with their fear of rejection, they make the mistake of trying to deal with the rejection itself. The problem is, that's not where the fear comes from. I see your eyebrows rising. Well, just hear me out for a moment. To find out where this fear comes from, let's walk back to your office. Leave the door open behind you and sit down for a second. I'll stand, thank you.

Now imagine that you're hard at work, and out of the blue there is a lot of noise coming from somewhere down the hallway. Can't get any work done, right? Why not? Ahh, the noise! What are you going to do about it? Right, get rid of the noise. Take the easy way — close the door. *Slam!* The reason you couldn't work is that you were distracted by the noise down the hall. It was keeping you from doing important things that had to get done. That noise has a lot in common with your fear of rejection.

Your fear of rejection is a distraction that keeps you from making successful telephone sales calls.

Rather than deal with the rejection, you should be handling the *distraction,* because that's what is throwing you off. What do we do with distractions? We get rid of them! While you can't shut the door on rejection, you have another less physical option: *Don't be surprised.*

Expect that some calls will not work out. I don't mean to imply that you should wish upon yourself a self-fulfilling prophecy, "I told you the person wouldn't be interested." On the contrary, just don't be surprised if you get turned down, because you will. Everyone does at one time or another. (The goal is to learn to be turned down less often.) *The act of anticipating that some calls won't work out eliminates distraction.* You can't be thrown off by something you expect to happen and are prepared to deal with.

The next time someone turns you down, you won't be mortally wounded, uttering, "They hung up on me!" You will have already anticipated that this would happen on occasion (although, at the time, you were focused on doing everything right to make the call succeed). The reason you won't feel rejected is that you will be prepared to deal with it in a positive manner. You will take this bad encounter and create a learning experience from it, because every time you learn, you become wiser, better, and, not surprisingly, more successful.

2. Change your thinking
Being prepared means knowing how to respond in a positive manner to anticipated rejection. You should be able to take something potentially negative and turn it into a proactive learning experience.

Here's a very effective way to do this:

When you are turned down, ask yourself, "Is it them or me?"

That simple little question is a powerful self-assessment trigger that instantly initiates self-assessment behavior. Self-assessment is the ability to identify where a mistake was made and the problems it caused, in order to prevent it from happening again. Self-assessment is probably the most overlooked business practice today, which is astounding considering that it is the fundamental activity for raising performance. Let me put it to you this way: Can you imagine the impact (on sales and customer satisfaction) if in just this week alone everyone in your organization stopped repeating their mistakes? Awesome! By asking the question, "Is it them or me?" you can automatically go into your self-assessment mode and resolve the problem in a positive, constructive manner.

It's that simple. If the answer you reach is that it's *them*, there is little you can do. The person you are calling might be having a bad day, might be distracted by a million other things and your call was simply ill-timed, or the individual is not as smart a business person as they think they are, because they don't entertain new ideas. It's not your job to change these people or the situation, just to know if it's them as opposed to you.

If it's *you*, use this as a celebration of learning. Success comes from learning where you went wrong and not making the same mistake twice.

I can appreciate that the very word "mistake" carries a negative connotation. For many people a mistake implies failure, and yet the irony is that mistakes are not a sign of failure, but of success, because mistakes are prerequisites for success. There isn't a billionaire on the planet who hasn't made mistakes. The secret to their success is that they didn't repeat them. Failure is the act of repeating mistakes. So it's fine to make a mistake, just not twice.

That's a lesson that was well learned by a financial consultant named Jeff out in Vancouver. Before this bright, enthusiastic fellow first attended one of my training programs, he was making sixty calls a day and booking only one appointment out of all those calls. (Who has time to see clients when you spend all day on the phone?) The appointments yielded $50,000 in assets per month. Once Jeff began training on this system, everything changed. In the first week he was booking one appointment out of every twenty calls. That increase was due to the fact that he immediately self-assessed where he was going wrong and fixed each problem, one problem at a time. For example, in the first day Jeff asked "Is it them or me?" and, realizing it was him, sat down to figure out what he was doing wrong.

What he discovered was that he was talking too fast (one of the main reasons why people will end their conversation with you). So Jeff wrote "SLOW" on a tent card on his desk as a visual reminder and slowed down, hence the increased results. He continued self-assessing after each call. As a result, by the end of the month Jeff was closing ten appointments out of every twenty calls. By six weeks he was at twelve for twenty. Now here's where the story gets interesting. This increased benchmark meant that Jeff ended up making only four calls a day (rather than sixty) and closed $500,000 a month in assets. That's a ten-fold increase in assets at a fraction of the calls. As you can see, self-assessment not only results in increased sales, but also delivers significant productivity gains. At the end of the day, this is not about making lots of calls, it's about making successful calls.

So the next time a call does not work out, for whatever reason, change your thinking. Think of each call as a *valuable resource*. Focus on your success so that the next time you make a telephone sales call that doesn't work out, ask yourself, "What can I learn from this?" Right there you will have created an opportunity to make winning sales calls.

Your reaction will shift from "I am surprised" to "I was expecting that," from "I feel rejected" to "What can I learn to become more successful?" Your focus will then shift from devastation to opportunity.

By changing your thinking, you change your outcome from inaction to action, from missing opportunities to opening new doors, from not making any more calls to making more successful telephone sales calls.

When you believe that every sales call is a good sales call because you learn from each one, calls that don't work out become valuable resources that can be analyzed and used to improve your performance and achieve your goals.

You change your expectations from a negative outcome (rejection, inaction) to a positive outcome (learning, making more successful calls).

Changing your expectations changes your attitude from negative and defeatist to positive and confident.

Your positive attitude affects your behavior: from inaction and paralysis to making more calls. The more calls you make, the more successful you become, building ever more confidence from learning and applying what you have learned.

Psychology 101 teaches us that any activity that gets rewarded gets done. So to get you in the habit of learning from your mistakes, you need to get into the habit of rewarding yourself for learning from your mistakes. This is not to be confused with rewarding yourself for making mistakes. It's the "learning" from your mistakes that you want to reward. A reward can be something as simple as a shoeshine, a long lunch, giving a few bucks to charity, or bringing home a treat for your spouse.

A while back a sales professional named Gordon told me that for the first week he was applying this system he gave his wife a single rose each night as a reward for learning from his mistakes. "We're getting better every day," he told his wife, in recognition that she too played a big role in his success. By the end of the week his wife had collected a handsome bouquet of roses. The following Monday Gordon came home with another rose. Tuesday night arrived with Gordon and no rose. In fact, there were no roses for the rest of the week. By Thursday Gordon was getting funny looks from his wife, who finally confronted him on Friday, wondering why he had stopped bringing her roses. Gordon told her that he had stopped making mistakes and hence, no reward for learning from his mistakes. That did little to comfort her, until he took out a pad and paper and worked through the numbers to show her what they stood to gain by way of a bonus for the potential new business he was about to land.

Time for a quick recap. The next time someone turns you down or is not interested, here's how you change your thinking.

Old Way of Thinking	New Way of Thinking
• You feel surprised.	• You have anticipated the response and are prepared.
• You feel rejected, devastated.	• You are looking forward to a learning experience.
• You ask yourself, "Why me?"	• You ask yourself, "Is it them or me?"
• Some calls are a waste of time and you are only going to be turned down.	• Every telephone sales call is a good call you can learn from.
• Mistakes are devastating.	• Mistakes are valuable resources.
• Despondent	• Confident
• Negative	• Positive
• Stop making calls	• Make more calls
• Defeatist	• Opportunistic
• You're not successful	• Making calls makes you successful.

Take a moment and go back to the last call you made where someone said they weren't interested. Tell me, was it them or was it you? Either the prospect was genuinely not interested because they had no requirement for your product or service — in which case they were doing you a favor by not wasting any more of your time — or it was something you said, or the way you said it. If it was them, there was nothing else you could have done anyway, and you can't take that personally.

If it was you, what did you learn?

_____

_____

_____

How can you challenge yourself to apply what you learn in the next series of calls?

_____

_____

_____

_____

What will your reward be?

_____

_____

_____

3. Reduce the possibility of being turned down

One sure way to eliminate your fear of rejection is by giving people no cause to turn you down in the first place. As I mentioned earlier, learning from your mistakes is one way to achieve this. But there are three other innovative strategies to accomplish the same goal. I call them the Caller Critique, the Find 'n' Fix It Audit, and the Objections Portfolio.

Caller Critique

If you had a crystal ball and could see all the calls you'll be making in the future, what mistakes would you see?

Why not prevent them from happening in the first place? One way to do that is to find out what other people are doing wrong and then learn from their mistakes. Learn by example.

Where to start? How about all those sales calls that you get at home or at the office from telemarketers? There's enough free research material there to fill up a library. Take advantage of it. Every time a call comes in, keep track of the telemarketer's performance. When you turn people down, or hang up on them, make a list of why you rejected other salespeople's pitches when they called you. What you will discover will be invaluable. You will begin to see your own errors in the mistakes of others. This will draw your attention to things like poor delivery (when people sound like they're reading from a script), lack of enthusiasm, lack of product knowledge, bad timing, bad scripting, lack of scripting, etc.

Let's get you organized so that you can keep track of this vital information. I want you to use a simple, effective system that I call the Caller Critique. Basically, it's a series of questions that you keep on a sheet of paper by the telephone, ready to be filled in the next time you get a telephone solicitation. Copy the Caller Critique (on the next page) and use it.

You'd be surprised at what you can learn from this simple exercise. The more information you have, the more you can analyze. All you have to do to improve your own performance is to see the mistakes in others and make a point of not repeating them. Over time you will find yourself making fewer and fewer mistakes as you practise this exercise in self-improvement.

A software rep named Tom told me that in the first week he kept this Caller Critique by his phone, he received a call from a phone company. Tom told the caller that they had already called him the previous week, to which the telemarketer replied, "You're wrong." Well, as you can imagine, Tom wasn't pleased. He told me that while he

Caller Critique

1. The telemarketer called
❏ In the middle of work ❏ Late in the evening
❏ At an acceptable time but I was busy ❏ At a bad time

2. How did the telemarketer come across in the first few seconds?
❏ Aggressive ❏ Pushy ❏ Rushed ❏ Lethargic ❏ Insincere
❏ Impersonal ❏ Other: _____
Reason: _____

3. The opening line was
❏ Unconvincing ❏ Vague ❏ Tired ❏ Insincere ❏ Awkward
❏ Unoriginal ❏ Uninspiring ❏ Irrelevant to me
❏ Other: _____
Reason: _____

4. How was the telemarketer's delivery?
❏ Unnatural ❏ Unenthusiastic ❏ Rushed ❏ Unprofessional
❏ Sounded too much like a script ❏ Didn't enunciate clearly
❏ No pauses/time to ask questions ❏ Too slow ❏ Low in energy
❏ Showed lack of confidence ❏ Other: _____

5. The telemarketer's voice was
❏ Too soft ❏ Too loud ❏ Tense ❏ Other: _____

6. The telemarketer's unique selling proposition
❏ Took a few minutes to figure out ❏ Still isn't clear
❏ Didn't benefit me/my company

7. How did the person listen to my comments?
❏ Partially ❏ Not at all ❏ Cut me off

8. How were my questions answered?
❏ Reluctantly ❏ Rudely ❏ Hurriedly
❏ Not all questions answered (some were side-stepped)
❏ Not all questions answered (caller didn't have all the answers)
❏ The telemarketer was clueless about the product/service offered

9. I lost interest
❏ Immediately ❏ After the opening line
❏ After my first question ❏ After my second question

Comments
_____
_____
_____
_____

had never told anyone he was calling that they were wrong, he was not about to start, since he now knows how angry people feel in that situation. Tom also made sure to double-up on his efforts to keep good records of those he spoke to and when. This learning exercise cost him nothing but could result in many new clients just by preventing such mistakes from ever happening.

Learning from others also means learning from what they do right. Anytime you find yourself saying yes to a demonstration of some product, or a salesperson coming to see you, or a sale of any product or service, the person calling you must have said something in a way that got your attention, got you to listen, and got you to take action! Keeping a separate list of what they said or did that motivated you will show you how a successful sales call is executed, and inspire you to do the same.

Calls That Impressed You

_____

_____

_____

_____

This reminds me of a story about a very good telemarketer who called me one day, asking if I'd be interested in having my broadloom cleaned. He was friendly, persuasive, knowledgeable, sincere. He delivered a good opening line and was generally very enthusiastic. I liked this fellow so much I really wanted to give him some business, but couldn't. You see, I don't have broadloom — just hardwood floors and area rugs. He offered then to clean my stairs (where there is broadloom), but I had just had the carpet installed a few months before and it was really quite clean. Well, wouldn't you know it, this guy then offered to clean the upholstery in my car and, believe me, I would have obliged the fellow if I could, but unfortunately I have a leather interior! But what a great effort! I know that telemarketer was truly professional in his outlook and attitude, and far from feeling rejected, I am certain he felt that it was a job well done under the circumstances.

Find 'n' Fix It Audit

There are two types of mistakes: those you know about, and those you don't. When you ask yourself, "Is it me?" you have some idea where you may have gone wrong: You didn't motivate yourself properly, you didn't sound natural enough or have enough energy or enthusiasm, etc. But every once in a while you will say or do something to adversely affect a call in a way that is not obvious right away. That's dangerous, because you might make the same mistakes over and over again and not even know it. It's kind of a vicious circle; since you don't know you're making mistakes, you keep making them. It's these subtle errors that I'm most concerned about, because they're the ones that do the most damage.

You can't fix a leaky pipe — even a pinhole leak — if you don't know where the leak is coming from.

What I have noticed over the years is that mistakes are as individual as the people who make them. Mistakes are very personal, and "personal" mistakes are harder to uncover. For example, you might not perform well on Mondays whereas others do. You might be less alert after a heavy lunch while others are fine. Or you may find that it takes you longer to get used to changes in your environment — a new desk, for example — while other people are unaffected by change. You could go on for years and never associate these problems with unsuccessful calls. Since every call is important, it is essential that you find the root cause of all your mistakes and fix them straight away.

I've developed an innovative technique for finding these personal mistakes, called the Find 'n' Fix It Audit. Before I explain it, let me tell you a true story of the unusual way I came about the idea.

Find 'n' Fix It Audit

1. Time of day I started making calls from my Hit List: _____

2. Time of day this particular call took place: _____

3. Day of the week: _____

4. Number of calls I made up until this call: _____

5. Number of people who turned me down up until this call: _____

6. Length of call: _____

7. What I did before the call to prepare for it:

_____

_____

_____

8. What I said:

_____

_____

_____

_____

9. What my prospect said:

_____

_____

_____

10. Changes to the script: ❑ Yes   ❑ No

11. How well I delivered my script:
❑ Poor   ❑ Fair   ❑ Good   ❑ Very Good   ❑ Excellent

12. How well I handled objections:
❑ Poor   ❑ Fair   ❑ Good   ❑ Very Good   ❑ Excellent

13. Posture:
❑ Slouching   ❑ Sitting up straight

14. Whether I was standing or sitting at the time
    I placed the call:
❑ Standing   ❑ Sitting

15. Where I was standing or sitting at the time I placed the call:

_____

16. The kind of activities that other people were doing around me:

_____

_____

_____

17. Any changes around the office:

_____

_____

_____

18. Number of breaks: _____

19. Break activities:

_____

_____

_____

20. Number of meals I've had today: _____

21. What I ate:
❏ Nothing   ❏ Snack   ❏ Light meal   ❏ Average meal
❏ Heavy meal   ❏ Junk food   ❏ Alcohol   ❏ Sweets

22. What I wore:

_____

23. The number of cups of coffee I've had today: _____

24. The number of distractions I've had between calls: _____

25. The kinds of distractions I've had between calls:

_____

_____

_____

26. Other pressures affecting me:

_____

_____

27. I notice a lack of:
❏ Energy   ❏ Enthusiasm   ❏ Focus

Allergies are nothing to sneeze at, and many years ago I was having a lot of pretty nasty allergic reactions. Problem was, I didn't have the foggiest notion what I was allergic to. Neither did my doctor. Fortunately for me, my allergist had an unorthodox approach to allergy testing. Rather than give me the usual six-hundred-needles-in-the-arm-but-don't-worry-this-won't-hurt-a-bit treatment, my doctor told me that every time I had a reaction from now on, I was to write down what I ate, what I wore, and what I was doing on that particular day. Over time I noticed a pattern developing for those days that I was reacting; I always had something with sugar in it, or I was around cigarette smoke. As it turns out, I'm allergic to both.

The reason why I'm telling you this personal information is that I learned to apply this technique to telephone sales calls. The next time a call doesn't work out as planned, and you ask yourself, "Is it them or is it me?" and the answer is *you*, only you don't know where you went wrong, fill out the Find 'n' Fix It Audit *immediately* after the call and keep it on file. Every time you have a similar experience, complete another Find 'n' Fix It Audit. After filling out half a dozen or so over time, you will see a pattern developing from a number of varied sources: either you did something differently than you normally do, your mistakes were made at the same time of the day or week or month, you reached a threshold where you burned out after a certain number of calls, you wore clothing that didn't motivate you, you changed your eating habits, perhaps outside factors were the root cause, etc. Whatever the problem, and wherever it comes from, you'll find it in your Find 'n' Fix It Audit. Once you can isolate your Achilles' heel, you can correct the matter and watch your success rate improve.

When you identify a recurring problem, write it down on a separate sheet, in large letters, so that you can look at it every day and remind yourself not to make the same mistake again. For example, say that you discover that under the question "Number of calls I made up until this call," you wrote "30" on several occasions. That pattern would suggest that you have a saturation point of thirty calls. In other words, after every thirty calls you either get tired and lose focus, or you remain focused but get over-confident and become careless. You should write down in large, bold letters:

30 CALLS . . . TAKE A BREAK!

I guarantee you won't make that mistake again. Naturally, your success rate will improve. As for rejection — you won't give it a second thought.

Objections Portfolio

What do you suppose would happen if you were to ignore a customer's questions and just keep rambling on with your sales pitch? Would that make the customer want to continue listening? If you don't have any good answers to the questions put to you, or worse, you bluff your way through them and the customer knows it, is there any hope of getting the appointment? Questions aside, people are bound to raise objections as to why they can't see you or do business with you. How far would your appointments and sales go if you had no effective response?

Anticipating objections and questions reduces your chances of being turned down.

Be fully prepared to answer any question or objection that may come along. Don't confuse legitimate questions with objections. Everyone, including yourself, asks questions about the things they buy. On occasion, you have legitimate objections or concerns, too (the cost is too much, it's not a good time, etc.). It's all a natural part of the process. So once again, the key is not to be surprised, and therefore distracted, when someone asks you questions or raises an objection. Knowing how to handle objections and answer questions keeps you in control. (Control builds confidence.) The ability to answer questions effectively without hesitation also builds trust (you come across like you know what you're talking about), and trust is the foundation of any relationship.

To help you plan your responses, there are four categories of objections to take into account:

- *Money*   • *Lack of information*
- *Competition*   • *Time*

Whenever someone asks you a question, acknowledge what was said, and then respond with a positive, passionate reply. The person will either respond with an objection from one of the four categories or will say "I'm not interested," at which point it's up to you to find out why, in order to determine which objection(s) you need to respond to.

When someone says "I'm not interested," a good response would be, "I can appreciate that, Mr. Schwartz, but please help me understand *why* you're not interested. Is it because you . . ." (Complete the sentence based on what you feel would be the main reason they're not interested.) When the person responds, you will have opened up a dialogue and will be prepared to answer their true objection. For example, they may respond with "We have a supplier," which is nothing more than a competition objection. Naturally, you will have an effective pat answer at hand to bring the person closer to booking the appointment.

Money:

When this a concern, you'll hear something like, "You're too expensive" or "We don't have any budget" or "We're in the middle of doing budgets." Explain that you are in the business of saving people money and improving productivity, or some other value proposition (whatever it is that makes your service or product worth the money).

When I was in advertising and someone said that they didn't have a budget, my response was, "I can appreciate that, Mr. Smith, but I like to see people well before they need me so that whenever a problem arises they know I'm available to solve it. When would be a good time to see you?" When told that I'm too expensive I would reply, "That's true, Mr. Smith, my services do not come cheap, but the value my clients receive for their money lies in my ability to nail a problem the first time around, deliver money-making concepts, and save them additional time and money by eliminating the need for costly revisions. I'd love to deliver the same value for you, Mr. Smith. When would be a good time to see you?"

Competition:

You'll hear, "We have a supplier" or "We do that in-house." I remember, when I was a freelance advertising copywriter, the one objection I was always sure to hear was, "We already have an agency." Did I panic or feel rejected? No way. I wasn't taken by surprise. I anticipated that remark, and was prepared to respond. My pat answer was, "That's great but, you know, all my customers had agencies before they met me and felt they were doing just fine, but chose to work with me because of my ability to handle difficult assignments. And I'd like to have the opportunity to do the same for you." It worked wonderfully well. If you've encountered a situation where someone says that they already receive your service in-house or by another supplier, explain how you can fill a gap in their needs. Be prepared to ask a question yourself to uncover a niche opportunity. For example, I sometimes asked, "Do your writers simplify complex technical information?"

Lack of Information:

Sometimes people you are calling simply need more information to make them feel comfortable that this is a good investment of their time. That's fine. Anticipate all the things people might ask, usually facts and figures, and keep your information at hand. If they ask you to send literature, that's your call. As a general rule I don't send information, because most of the time it ends up being chucked away in some dusty cabinet marked, "Time Capsule. Do Not Open Until 2410." If someone can't make the decision to see me, I haven't given them a good enough reason to see me.

Having said that, there are times when it pays to send information, mostly when the prospect is located out of town, time and money are issues, and/or the potential value of your contract is too low to warrant the time required, making you want to pre-qualify the prospect a little further. In those instances, be prepared ahead of time to send the information via fax, e-mail, or courier. Faster is better but, as a rule of thumb, ask the prospect which mode of communication they prefer. Whichever route you take, make sure to schedule a follow-up call one week later. Don't assume anyone will call you back, even if they are interested. It's your responsibility to take control and show initiative.

If possible, have all your information on your Website so that prospects can review the information in real time. It makes it easier and quicker for your prospects to distribute your information to their peers.

Since you already have your prospect on the telephone, book an appointment with them anyway in the form of a follow-up call. This way, rather than see the person face to face, you will speak with the individual over the phone at a future date to discuss the information you are sending. Once you get a confirmed day and time, record it in a separate Call Memo, which you will use to keep track of follow-up calls.

Time:

You might really be calling at a bad or inopportune time (budget reviews). Before you ask when the best time to call back would be, you might want to say something like, "I like to see people well before they need my services, so that when the need arises, you'll already know that I can solve your problem." Quite often, as soon as people sense that you are not in hurry and this is no hard sell, they say, "Come on in."

If the timing really isn't good, you might consider something like, "Would it be of value to call you in a few months in the event that your situation changes?" This respectful approach allows you to leave the conversation sounding like a consummate professional, while at the same time picking up some business when the timing is good. It's happened to me on many occasions.

Another interesting subtlety is the use of the word "value." By saying "would it be of value?" you are implying that conversations with you have value. When someone gives you the go-ahead to call them, ask which month they would prefer you to call, and then thank them for their time. When you call them back you are now calling as requested, which you can mention to the person's assistant. You might begin your conversation with, "When we spoke last January you requested that I call you back now to review your situation."

Sometimes people who don't want to take the time to see you may just ask you for a quote. Unless you are offering a commodity, there is always value that you bring to the table, and you need to articulate that value. Your role is to find out not what prospects want (they'll tell you what they want), but what they need. Someone might want a cheap flight to the coast when what they need instead is a direct flight to the coast (with legroom, please). Let the person know that in order to do the right job for them, you want to make sure you are giving them exactly what they need. Here's an example.

"I'd be happy to give you a quote, but I really believe that I'm going to do a better job for you by first understanding the commitments you have to *your* customers. That way I'm in a position not only to give you the best price — which I know you want — but also to share with you some important options you may never have considered. That's the value I bring to the table, and that's why I feel it's important that we meet. When would be a good time?"

One very important aspect of effectively responding to questions and objections is listening to exactly what is being asked or said. Here's an example. Suppose you were a financial advisor and someone told you that they already use the services of one of your competitors. Here are three possible objections with very subtle differences: "I already have an advisor." "I have a relationship with (competing firm)." "I've been with (competing firm) for over twenty years." In the first objection the prospect is telling you that they have an advisor. In the second remark they are telling you that a relationship is in place with a specific firm. In the third response they are telling you that a long-standing relationship is firmly carved in stone and will not be moved. By listening for these subtleties you can instantly customize your response to exactly what is being said. Here are a few examples.

"I already have an advisor."
"I'd be surprised if you didn't have an advisor. You know, ninety-five percent of our clients have two or three relationships with other financial advisors, but retain our services to gain exclusive access to new investment ideas, stock options, and estate-planning innovations that they would normally not be privy to. Which is exactly what I'd like to offer you. When can we meet?"

"I have a relationship with (competitor)."

"I'm sure you have an excellent relationship. (Competitor) is a first-class firm, which is why many of our clients also maintain a relationship with them, while at the same time relying on us to stay on top of new investment ideas, stock options, and estate-planning innovations that only we have access to. Which is exactly why a person of your wealth should have a relationship with (your firm). When can we meet?"

"I've been with (competitor) for many years."

"I'm glad you're well looked after, and I'm not here today to replace that relationship at all, but rather to enhance it, just as we've done for a lot of our clients who also maintain an excellent relationship with (competitor). What I'm offering is an opportunity to keep your options open by giving you access to new investment ideas, stock options, and estate-planning innovations that (competitor) does not currently offer. Which is exactly why a person of your wealth should have an additional relationship with (your firm). When can we meet?"

Notice how in the second response the competing firm was recognized and addressed, and in the third response (where the relationship was carved in stone), the issue was defused immediately and firmly. At the end of each response there was a passionate request to meet in person.

Take a moment and list your favorite objections that *you* use on telemarketers.

_____

_____

_____

_____

_____

Now list the possible objections/questions you anticipate hearing when *you* make telephone sales calls and note any subtleties.

1. _____

2. _____

3. _____

4. _____

5. _____

Write your best responses to those objections and questions in the Objections Portfolio. As you do, apply this simple four-step process: First acknowledge what was said, then defuse the issue, say something unique or compelling, and then passionately ask for the appointment.

Objections Portfolio

• Money   • Competition   • Lack of Information   • Time

Objection/Question:
_____
_____

Response:
_____
_____
_____
_____

Objection/Question:
_____
_____

Response:
_____
_____
_____
_____

As you begin making calls, you will undoubtedly experience objections and questions that you have not anticipated. But you won't be surprised or taken aback, right? Since every call is a good call when you learn something from it, you will welcome the learning experience and add the new objections and questions to your Objections Portfolio, better prepared for the next time. Each time you apply what you learn you will be making yourself more successful.

Having good, time-tested responses will also pay handsomely in your face-to-face encounters. A financial consultant named Leo told me just how much it can come in handy. Leo is sitting in a meeting when out of the blue the prospective client gives him the mother of all objections (for financial advisors): "We already have a broker and we've been working with him for fifteen years and, oh yeah, he's my brother-in-law." Now you and I both know that this person was testing Leo, otherwise they would never have arranged the meeting in the first place. But Leo was prepared. He told me that normally he would have been defensive right then and there, but instead he was confident.

In fact, he went on "autopilot," because he had written and rehearsed a good response that he could deliver passionately and without hesitation. The result? The prospect cut Leo a check for $600,000. Leo walked out of there with close to $38,000 in commission. And here's the best part: this was three days before his wedding. What a wonderful gift.

4. Stay focused on success

When I was looking for my first job in advertising back in 1980, I did not know of the existence of executive search people. Instead, I sent résumés to over fifty advertising agencies, and followed up each one with a telephone call. Time after time I got turned down, but I persevered. After my forty-fifth call and rejection, my best friend, Stephen

Cohen, and I headed off to our customary ice cream place for a therapeutic injection of calories and encouragement. He turned to me and asked, "What keeps you going?" My reply was instinctive: "I figure that every person who turns me down brings me closer to the one who says yes." Sure enough, on my fiftieth call I landed a job at a terrific agency. The moral of this true story is that rather than focus on the rejection I focused on success. My motto was powerful:

Every caller that turns you down brings you closer to the one that says yes.

I knew that the more calls I made, the better my chances of success. Each call *you* make will bring you closer to reaching your goals and dreams too. So never lose sight of where you're going. Keep your focus on your objectives. You already know that feeling rejected is a form of distraction that takes your focus away from where you want to go. You know that every sales call is a good sales call, when you learn from it. The important thing is to stay focused on making your calls successful and, as you do, keep your sights on your overall success. The big picture. The reason why you're doing all this. Your ultimate destination. In other words, the collective end result of making all those calls.

Try this little exercise for a moment:

Imagine that you are a general in an army in the midst of an all-out war. After spending months planning a particularly complex campaign, you go to battle, only to find yourself defeated in the first engagement. What are you focused on next?

_____

_____

_____

_____

Describe your next step.

_____

_____

_____

_____

_____

Every single person who has tried this has answered that, as a general, they would be focused on winning the next battle. The answer that will make you a more decorated general: Stay focused on winning the war! Your next step will be to accomplish that goal by learning from the mistakes you made in the battle you lost. If you focus on defeat, you'll end up defeated. If you focus on winning the war, you won't be set back by the inevitable defeats along the way, because you anticipate they will happen (sound familiar?) and will not be sidetracked from your main objective: total victory.

Before you can focus on success, you have to have a clear picture of what success means to you. Define success.

_____

_____

_____

_____

_____

Since you move in the direction of the visions you create, take a moment and **draw what success means to you**.

That's your main focus. As a result, you are only interested in calls that are successful. That means you are willing to learn from every call, and move yourself forward towards achieving your goal. Who has time for rejection when you're on your way to success!

Fear of Failure

Many people hold themselves back from success because they are afraid of failing. I'd like to set the record straight right now and tell you that with sales calls there is no such thing as failure.

When you make telephone sales calls, you cannot fail. Every time you make a sales call you make success possible: You improve your performance. You are closer to a sale. You increase your opportunities. (Even if you only get one appointment today you are measurably more successful than if you didn't make any sales calls at all.) The act of making calls will in itself ensure your success.

You never fail when taking steps to ensure your success.

It's only when you *don't* make sales calls that you invite failure, because you diminish your chances for success. *If you are truly afraid of failure, then you should really be afraid of not making sales calls.* If you do not make use of the telephone to reach your objectives, then you are failing to live up to your full potential. You are doing yourself a gross injustice. You have the means to do anything you want, achieve the highest goals possible, if only you make the effort. Plain and simple. When you make a telephone sales call and it doesn't pan out, that's not failing, in my book. *Not making the call at all is failure.* You are deliberately sabotaging your success. Make the calls and success will follow.

The action of making a sales call is in itself a measure of your success.

Après Fear

After you have had the time to apply what you have learned in this chapter, dig into your memory and recall the first positive image you drew at the beginning of this section — you know, the one where I asked, "If you were not afraid to make telephone sales calls, what would you be, and what would be different?" Don't look at it in the book. Recall it in your mind. (It should be engraved there forever.) You should already feel yourself moving in the direction of that image. How does it feel? Hector and Orestes would be proud of you.

3

Call Planning

*I*f I gave you a list of twenty very busy people to call, how many people would you reach? (Aha. I was afraid you were going to say that.)

Every single call you make is important.

I refer to a call as a Ming dynasty vase. Handle it carefully and with respect. In fact, this system is all about respecting yourself, respecting the person you are calling, and respecting the call itself.

You cannot afford to miss a single individual. How many calls do you give up on or forget about because they've dragged on for weeks on end? If you answered even "one," that's one too many. That could be the one prospect that could change your career. The one contact that opens countless other opportunities for you. The largest contract you've ever had.

Let's play a little game here. I'm thinking of a number from one to a hundred. Guess what number?

Not even close. Guess again . . .

Last chance.

Sorry.

It was unfair of me to ask, right? You're not a mind reader. Come to think of it, neither am I. That's why no one can ever know with certainty exactly which call will result in a sale, a referral, new business opportunities, or phenomenal contacts. That means that you have to reach *everyone* on your list. You can't skip a single call.

I have invented something called the Fallen Call Theory (for calls that have fallen through the cracks), which states that the domino effect from missing a single call can cost your business a fortune over time (often in as little time as one year).

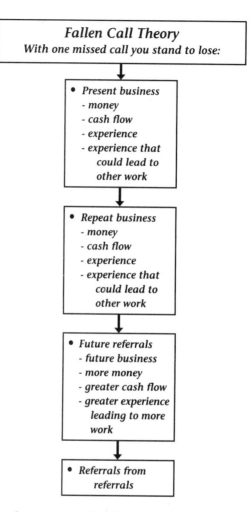

Fallen Call Theory
With one missed call you stand to lose:

- *Present business*
  - *money*
  - *cash flow*
  - *experience*
  - *experience that could lead to other work*

- *Repeat business*
  - *money*
  - *cash flow*
  - *experience*
  - *experience that could lead to other work*

- *Future referrals*
  - *future business*
  - *more money*
  - *greater cash flow*
  - *greater experience leading to more work*

- *Referrals from referrals*

That's what you stand to lose by not getting through to just one single prospect. A few seconds with a calculator will tell the rest of that horror story.

Getting hold of decision makers is one of the biggest challenges people face, and yet it's one of the easiest things to turn around. My experience has shown that people typically miss seventy-five percent of their opportunities just because they don't speak with prospects live on the phone. You want to make sure that you uncover not only your biggest opportunities, but also the low-hanging fruit. I had one client who got an appointment without even finishing his sentence. As soon as he mentioned the name of his company, the prospect jumped in and said, "I've been wanting to see your company." Never run past a motivated buyer with his wallet out.

If you master only this section on Call Planning and walk away without applying the rest of this system, your results will go up. But stick around for the rest. Other than measuring your Reach (ability to contact people), you must also make a point of measuring your Effectiveness (how good you are at securing an appointment once you are speaking with your prospect).

It's interesting to note here a major sacred cow of telemarketing — that we live in an infinite world. I'm sure you've worked for someone at one time who said, "Here's a list of a thousand people, just call them. There's more when you're done." I have an alternative view — that we live in a finite world. There are only so many people you can call who are qualified to do business with you. Hence every encounter has to be a positive one. Even if the timing is off, at least you will have left the door open to call back when the timing is better.

Another sacred cow of telemarketing is that the objective is making calls. The reality is that the objective is getting appointments. If all you want to do is make calls, why not just get your hands on a great big phone book and call, call, call! The objective is not to make lots of calls but to make successful calls. (You also want to book more appointments with fewer calls to reap significant productivity gains.)

This system is not about volume. It's about precision. Focus on quality not quantity.

Now I know that you're sitting there thinking that getting hold of people is no easy task. People aren't sitting around at their desks waiting for you to call. (Wouldn't that be nice!) They have this nasty habit of moving around a lot, usually just before you call.

Trying to get hold of people with busy schedules is like trying to hit a moving target.

That's why most people simply give up after the first couple of attempts. However, with the right radar, anyone can zero in on a moving target, no matter how fast it is moving. My call planning techniques are kind of like radar: You close in on your target so that you reach everyone you want to call in the least amount of time. The less time the better, because the longer it takes you to reach people, the more likely you are to give up and skip a call — with your luck, it's the call of the century.

Spend your time talking to people, not chasing them.

Here's the strategy. I'd like you to change the way you make your calls now, from a hit-and-miss, on-and-off approach to one of a well orchestrated Call Campaign. This campaign consists of organizing and planning a series of calls, in groups of twenty or less, to maximize your ability to reach more people and make it easier to stay motivated.

If you're like most people, you get the name of a person to contact, rush over to the telephone (if you're motivated), and call up the company right away. After you ask the receptionist for your contact, your call is placed through — right through to the prospect's secretary, actually. (Secretaries are often referred to as administrative assistants. I refer to them simply as assistants.) Then what do you do? You're unprepared. You have to deal with a person you have never spoken to before, and have no time to feel that person out. (Friend or foe?) Or perhaps you are transferred instead directly to your prospect and again you're caught off guard and stumble over what you want to say, or you're thrown off by a rough-sounding voice or a thick accent you weren't expecting. You stumble, mumble, and lose the call.

To add insult to injury, the thought of repeating this kind of performance turns you off so much that you don't get around to making other calls for days on end. Then the days turn into weeks. Weeks turn into months. Still no calls?

From now on, plan every aspect of your call in advance.

The objective is to keep your eye on your calls. Know where your prospects are, or where they might be next. Anticipate and overcome every obstacle that can keep you from reaching people and reaching your goals.

I want to put you in a position of strength where you — not the receptionist, the assistant, or the prospect — are in control of the call process from start to finish. You alone take charge of the call. Simply knowing that you have the power to reach people consistently builds confidence, which enhances motivation. Whenever I call someone, I automatically assume that I'm going to reach them, no matter how busy they are or how impregnable their defenses. In fact, people are always saying, "I don't know how you got a hold of me. I'm never here." If you give me a list of twenty people to call, I will reach all twenty. You can too.

There is no mystery in tracking people down — there is only methodology.

Your Call Campaign is organized around the following six proven activities and tools that give you the power to reach any person, every time.

Call Planning Methodology
  1. Compile a Hit List
  2. Organize a Call Memo

3. Review a Receptionist Checklist
4. Examine an Assistant Checklist
5. Use the Voicefinder
6. Prepare a Hot-Call Travel Planner

(While the Call Planning methodology is primarily designed for reaching people at a business number, the Hit List and Call Memo components can be used effectively to reach residential customers. Although calling a residence requires considerably less organizing, it is still essential to plan your calls ahead of time, in groups of ten or more, as part of an overall Call Campaign.)

1. Hit List

If you're going to hit a moving target, you have to know what you're aiming at.

The Hit List is designed to keep track of who you are calling and where and when to reach them. The Hit List places essential call-planning information at your fingertips so that you don't misplace any critical call data, and organizes the information into a single campaign in advance of placing your calls. Here's what your Hit List looks like.

HIT LIST

Company name:	Company name:	Company name:
Prospect:	Prospect:	Prospect:
Title:	Title:	Title:
❏ Male ❏ Female	❏ Male ❏ Female	❏ Male ❏ Female
Phone Number:	Phone Number:	Phone Number:
Ext/Direct Line:	Ext/Direct Line:	Ext/Direct Line:
Time Zone:	Time Zone:	Time Zone:
Assistant/Phone:	Assistant/Phone:	Assistant/Phone:
Referral:	Referral:	Referral:
Time In:	Time In:	Time In:
Active:	Active:	Active:

Before you make a single call, complete your Hit List, and then *commit to it*. Use it as a visible goal with achievable results that will be rewarded. In other words, look at it as a challenge to reach all the names on the list, and when you finish each campaign, reward yourself for making all the calls.

Hit List Categories

(When you are calling on companies, complete all the categories in advance. If you are calling on residential customers, create a call campaign of ten or more calls using only the following three Hit List categories: Prospect, Number, and Referral.) Your first point of contact will be the receptionist, followed by the prospect's assistant and, finally, the prospect.

Company:

Verify the correct pronunciation of the company name with the receptionist.

> Company name:
> SJS Productions Inc.

Prospect:

Who do you want to talk to? If you don't already know, ask the receptionist. As soon as some receptionists hear you inquire about someone, they automatically assume that you want to speak to them right away, and connect you unannounced. That puts you out of control, and that's not where you want to be.

From the has-this-ever-happened-to-you category: You call up a company and ask the receptionist for the name of a particular prospect. Without telling you the person's name, the receptionist then places your call, either to the administrative assistant or directly to the prospect.

What can go wrong when you reach the assistant unprepared?

_____

What can go wrong when you reach the prospect unprepared?

_____

I wouldn't want to be in your shoes. Staying in control means that you find out who you want to speak to without being connected right away. To do that, here's what to say to the receptionist:

"Good morning! Could you please tell me the *name* of the individual who is in charge of . . ." (Place the emphasis on "name.")

Another thing to check is the correct pronunciation of your prospect's name, especially if the name is unfamiliar to you. (The name might be thirteen letters long, eleven of which are consonants.) There is nothing worse than mispronouncing someone's name. It's nothing that a Hit List couldn't prevent, so don't let it happen to you. Either ask the receptionist or call up your prospect's voicemail late at night to hear firsthand the pronunciation.

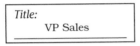

Prospect:
Rick (pronounced "reek") Patrick

Title:

Are you speaking with the correct person in the department? Again, if you don't know, ask the receptionist in advance.

Title:
VP Sales

Male/Female:

It's amazing how such a seemingly moot point can save your skin. Suppose someone tells you to call Pat so-and-so. Or Michel/le. Or Chris. Or Jean. If you think your prospect is female and a man answers the telephone, you are caught off guard and stand a good chance of losing the call. Ask the receptionist, or listen to the person's voicemail late at night to find out if you will be talking to a he or a she.

☑ *Male*   ❏ *Female*

Number:

Can you calculate how much time you will waste calling people up only to find out they are no longer at that number? Not to mention the negative effect of being distracted and losing your momentum. People move around a lot as they change jobs, positions, and offices, so it's a good idea to call ahead of time and just confirm with the receptionist that the number and extension you have is current. Don't speak to the prospect yet. Stay in control and continue down the list.

```
Phone Number:
   (000) 000-0000
```

Ext./Direct Line:

Obtain the extension or direct line from the receptionist; often, the administrative assistant is quite protective of the boss's direct line. (If the receptionist does not know, then proceed to ask the assistant.) The direct line and extension numbers are especially handy when you're trying to reach people who come into their office early in the morning before the switchboard is open. Most often these individuals can only be reached through their direct lines, because they are off in meetings the rest of the day. Again, there's a right way and a wrong way to ask for the extension number without having the receptionist place your call straight through to the prospect:

WRONG WAY

> You: Where can I reach Mr. Schwartz?
>
> Receptionist: I'll put you through . . .
>
> Before you can say, "I was only asking for his extension number ... ", you are on the line with Mr. Schwartz. (What do you say now?)

RIGHT WAY

> You: Good morning! I was wondering if you could please tell me the *extension number* of Mr. Schwartz? (Place the emphasis on "extension number.")

In the event you are unable to obtain the direct line from either the receptionist or assistant, try dialing another extension and asking the prospect's colleague for the direct line, or call after hours when the automated attendant may direct you to the company directory.

(One small footnote here: When you are ready to call a direct line, and it rings three times, hang up! Most likely the person isn't in, and the line is either connected to their voicemail or is routed to the assistant. Call back.)

| Extension: | Direct Line: |
| 424 | (000) 000-0000 |

Time Zone:

In a global business world you will likely be making more calls outside your city, to other parts of the country, or to other countries altogether. Thanks again to the ever dependable Hit List, you can properly plan for these calls by arranging them in order of time zones: one hour behind, two hours behind — or the other way around — one hour ahead, two hours ahead, etc. It's best to code them +1 (for one hour ahead) or –1 (for one hour behind). This way you'll know when to call and can schedule accordingly.

| Time Zone: |
| + 2 |

Administrative Assistant:

Assistants are wonderful people, and can be your greatest allies. Since you will have an opportunity to speak with them to ask for information (and stay in control), you will want to be as friendly as possible and strike an instant rapport. You can do that by saying hello and addressing the person by his or her first name. To that end, obtain the assistant's name from the receptionist in advance. You don't want to speak with the assistant just yet though; you only want to know the name and phone number.

Here's the correct way to ask the receptionist:

"Good afternoon! I was wondering if you could please tell me the *name* of Mr. Schwartz's assistant?" (Place the emphasis on "name.")

| Assistant: |
| Margaret |

Referral:

Referrals are like gold. They open doors and help you get the attention of your prospect. It's important to record your referrals on the Hit List so that you don't forget who was referred by whom and get your referrals mixed up. Hey, it happens.

| Referral: |
| Rod Brickman |

Time In:

The last time I looked up into the heavens, I noticed that the earth does not revolve around you and me. If it did, people we want to reach would be at their desks at the exact moment we call them. If you don't know ahead of time what time they can be reached, you will spend a lot of time chasing them, and end up frustrated and giving up. The good news is that people are creatures of habit. Some people come into the office at the same time every day: 7:30 a.m., 7:45, 8:00, or 8:15. If you know when your prospects routinely come in, you will be sure to reach them.

Always remember that the best time to reach someone is when they're in!

As you accumulate this call planning information, *prioritize your Hit List in the order in which people become available.* In other words, put the calls you have to make first — the early birds — at the top of the list, and those individuals who arrive in their office late, at the bottom of the list. It's the only way to ensure that you reach everyone, in the shortest time possible.

Find out from the receptionist the time when your prospect is expected to arrive in the morning. (Please do this even when you already have the prospect's direct line. A direct line only tells you *where* the person can be reached, not *when* they can be reached.)

> *You:* Good morning Susan, this is Steven Schwartz. I was wondering if you could tell me what time Tom usually arrives in the morning?

(I suppose you could also ask for the time when the prospect is going to arrive in that day, but if you don't reach the person right away you'll have to start all over again the following day. By knowing the time the person usually arrives to work in the morning, you are learning your prospect's habits, and habits tend to be very consistent things you can follow with accuracy.) If the receptionist doesn't know, ask the prospect's assistant. In the event that no one knows, or there is no receptionist or assistant to ask, complete the rest of the Hit List and then try this sure-fire technique, which I call *Closing the Window*: Call your prospect at 7:00 a.m., and then every fifteen minutes after that until 9:00, or until you hear that the person has changed their voice-mail greeting (assuming that your prospect is the type who changes their greeting every day). For example, if you call at 7:00 and the voicemail has yesterday's greeting, and then at 7:15 you hear today's greeting, you know that the person probably comes in between 7:00 and 7:15. Mark that down in your Hit List, and then the next day call back every few minutes within that time slot, because you know that the person will be coming in at any moment. Be prepared to speak with your prospect in the event that the person picks up the telephone during your probing. You will probably hear them say, "You just caught me coming in the door." If the person does not change their daily voice-mail greeting, simply close the time gap between calls each day (calling every fifteen minutes one day, then every ten minutes the next day, etc.) until you reach the person.

Another technique is to dial another extension number so that you can speak with someone who may have an office down the hall from the person you want to reach. They can tell you when the prospect is usually in, and if the person you want to reach is there at the time you call, you can get their colleague to transfer your call. (It will be seen as an internal call by your prospect.) If you feel your prospect is screening calls, call back before and after work hours, from 6:30 to 8:00 a.m. and from 6:00 to 8:00 p.m. People are not in "work mode" at those times and therefore tend not to be in "call screen" mode either. If you have tried all these techniques and you still can't reach the person, then as a last measure send an e-mail. To pique their interest, the message should be the same one that you will be delivering once you speak on the phone. (You'll learn how to write that script in the next section.) I have found this works well with people who are reflective by nature, and who prefer to express their words carefully through writing rather than speaking on the phone.

> *Time In:*
>   9:15 a.m.

Active:

Double check to make sure the person you are calling is in town, because if your prospect is away, you'll spin your wheels. Inquire from the receptionist, and if that person doesn't know, then ask the assistant or check late at night with the prospect's voicemail (they may have left a message saying they're out of town).

```
Active:
    Back on Tuesday
```

(Time out for a note: If you feel you have to ask the receptionist more than two questions, it's best to call back the next day and ask another few questions. The receptionist will not remember who you are, and will not mind answering a few questions for such a polite individual as yourself.)

Once you have completed all the categories in your Hit List and prioritized them in order of arrival, you are ready to begin your Call Campaign, fully in control of the situation. (Your confidence is up too, I notice.) Commence dialing.

2. Call Memo

If you're going to hit a moving target you have to know where it is at all times.

As you begin to make your calls from your Hit List, there will be some targets who slip through the cracks. Either they are late or they have a meeting away from the office, or perhaps there were several people arriving so close together on your list that you were bound to miss a few. Most people never follow up after the first attempt, and this is probably the main reason why they never reach anyone, and give up trying.

As you would expect, I have a tool for catching prospects who are not there when you call; it's called the Call Memo, and it allows you to track your prospects' whereabouts throughout the course of a day or week. It includes the same information as your Hit List, except for the last two categories; replace Time In and Active with Call Back and Comments. For example, suppose John Smith was originally expected in his office at 8:00, and when you called you discovered that he was delayed for two hours. Under the old way of doing things, you would get busy going about your business and forget about this person (and the opportunity) altogether. Your prospect not only fell through the cracks, he jumped into the Grand Canyon of lost calls. But I'm not going to let you lose anyone. Effective call planning is about reaching absolutely everyone.

Did I hear someone call for a Call Memo?

CALL MEMO

Company name:	Company name:	Company name:
Prospect:	Prospect:	Prospect:
Title:	Title:	Title:
❏ Male ❏ Female	❏ Male ❏ Female	❏ Male ❏ Female
Phone Number:	Phone Number:	Phone Number:
Ext/Direct Line:	Ext/Direct Line:	Ext/Direct Line:
Time Zone:	Time Zone:	Time Zone:
Assistant/Phone:	Assistant/Phone:	Assistant/Phone:
Referral:	Referral:	Referral:
Call Back:	Call Back:	Call Back:
Comments:	Comments:	Comments:

Call Back:

Find out from the assistant when, that day, the prospect is expected back.

> *You:* Hi Mary. It's Steven Schwartz calling back. You were kind enough to advise me that Gary would be arriving this morning around 8:00. Yet when I called he wasn't in, so I called back a few times until 8:30

> but without much luck. When would
> you advise would be a good time for me
> to catch up with him?

When you miss someone it's often just by a few minutes, so it's very important to know exactly when they're expected back. As a general rule of thumb, subtract fifteen minutes from whatever time the assistant gives you. If the assistant says that John Smith is expected back at 3:00, call back at 2:45. I can't explain exactly why this works, but over the years and thousands of calls, I find that more often than not people end up arriving on the early side.

Prioritize your Call Memo by the order in which people become available and then call back as scheduled. You'll find yourself reaching everyone faster.

(When calling residential customers: Should the person you are calling not be in and someone else answers the call, ask the person you are speaking with what time your prospect will be available, and then note that time in the Call Back category.)

> *Call Back:*
> 2:45

Comments:
Record any other valuable comments from the assistant that will help your cause, such as why the prospect is not available (really busy, conference call, out of town at the last minute, etc.).

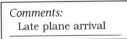

> *Comments:*
> Late plane arrival

Note: If you use personal information management software, incorporate your Hit List and Call Memo into your computer program. The prompting features in the software will enhance your effectiveness by reminding you when to call, and make it more convenient to update your Call Memo when travelling.

3. Receptionist Checklist

Receptionists are people too, so be just as courteous, friendly, and funny as with secretaries. Making their day will make yours as well. Before you call, know exactly why you want to speak with the receptionist:

- ❏ *Receptionist's name*
- ❏ *Correct pronunciation of the company name*
- ❏ *Name of prospect/contact*
- ❏ *Correct pronunciation of the prospect/contact name*
- ❏ *Official title of your contact*
- ❏ *Gender of your contact*
- ❏ *Confirm number*
- ❏ *Confirm extension number/direct line*
- ❏ *Assistant's name and number*
- ❏ *Best time to call the prospect*

Don't ask all at once. Call back on different days to get all the information you need, asking no more than three questions at a time.

4. Assistant Checklist

I've mentioned assistants several times by now. What you may not realize is that in every instance, I arranged for you to speak with the assistant deliberately. Since I'm a real control freak, and insist that *you stay in control of the call process at all times*, I never want to speak to an administrative assistant by accident, or by surprise. Every encounter with an assistant must be anticipated and planned.

It's funny how people tend to think that assistants are placed on Earth to get in your way, and that you have to avoid them at all costs. My experience has lead me to believe the opposite. Assistants are often your best allies. They have a wealth of valuable information, and the power to deliver your prospects to you, even when you can't reach the prospects yourself. On many occasions I've had assistants put me on hold while they went down the hall and got their bosses for me. Why do you suppose they did that?

Several reasons. First, I was in control of the call. I contacted them deliberately and for a specific purpose, and therefore came across as very confident. People respond well to anyone who exudes confidence. (For your edification, here's a simple equation about confidence: confidence = planning + positive attitude + control.) Second, I believed that the assistants were going to help me, and that expectation gave me a positive attitude, which translated itself into friendly behavior, which in turn was noticed by the assistants and reciprocated. It's that simple.

If, on the other hand, I had believed that assistants were nothing but obstacles, I would expect confrontation. That expectation would give me a negative attitude, which would come out in confrontational behavior, which would also be reciprocated in kind.

How do you feel about administrative assistants? Picture yourself calling a prospect, and the assistant answers the telephone.

Draw what this assistant reminds you of.

Now consider for a moment that you are an administrative assistant. List the kinds of things you have to put up with all day from people on the telephone.

_____

_____

_____

_____

As an assistant dealing with people on the telephone all day, what kinds of things could the people calling you do to make your day more enjoyable?

_____

_____

_____

_____

Now, having completed this checklist, **draw another impression of an assistant.**

```



```

Notice any difference between your first drawing and this last one? By the time you made your second drawing, you had developed empathy for the assistant's position. Not a bad way to build bridges of understanding and co-operation.

Now answer this: What's the most important word in the English language? Your name, right? Everyone likes to be called by their first name, including assistants. (Obtain the assistant's name from the receptionist before speaking with the assistant.) Using an assistant's first name also builds a warm rapport, because the person feels as if he or she knows you or has spoken with you before. By being proactive in calling the assistant and addressing that person on a first-name basis, you also dramatically reduce the chances of someone asking the reason for your call.

When calling on smaller companies you might run into a situation where there are no assistants, and the receptionist turns out to be the sole office secretary. You still need to be on a first-name basis right from the start, so begin with something like this:

> *You:* Good morning, who am I speaking with?
> *Receptionist:* Mary Jane. How may I direct your call?
> *You:* I need your help Mary. I was wondering if you could please tell me *the name* of your VP of sales.

If the receptionist is in fact the office secretary, add the receptionist's name to the Assistant column of your Hit List.

Mentioning any referrals right away also draws support, plus it adds a measure of endorsement and respectability to your cause. Should you not have any referrals to mention, and the assistant asks you why you are calling (although most of them won't), be honest, but be brief, confident, and enthusiastic. Something like this:

> *Assistant:* What is this regarding?
> *You:* (*Smiling*) Susan, I'm glad you asked that. I'm looking forward to speaking with Mr. Schwartz because I've been very successful in helping companies increase their performance benchmarks by over six hundred percent, and that's a subject that I know Mr. Schwartz is going to want to

> talk about in more detail. When would
> you advise would be a good time to speak
> with him?

There are three subtleties to observe here. The first is the phrase "I'm glad you asked," which creates an impression of supreme confidence. Notice too how the brief dialogue incorporated some sizzle from the telephone commercial you will be delivering when you speak with Mr. Schwartz (although you did not repeat the entire script). The third is the closing question where you ask for the assistant's advice. When was the last time an assistant was asked for advice? These subtleties will keep you in control and deliver the information you are requesting.

You can also try a slightly more advanced approach, which is one where you speak in terms the assistant can clearly relate to. For example, suppose the assistant's boss is a Chief Financial Officer:

Assistant: What is this regarding?

You: (Smiling) I'm glad you asked. I'm looking forward to speaking with Mr. Schwartz because as you know Susan, he's very concerned about his budget for next quarter, and I have found a way for him to recover about $10,000 from his equipment leasing that can free up some badly needed cash, and that's why I know he'll be quite anxious to speak to me about this. When would you advise would be a good time to speak with him?

The assistant can relate to the boss pacing in the office, anxious about cash flow and the budget. Notice the subtle use of the word "anxious."

If you really want to make the assistant's day, say good morning like you really mean it. Put lots of energy and enthusiasm into it. Anyone who comes across as friendly and energetic will be like a warm breeze on a spring day. The friendliness will be reciprocated in kind. Usually when assistants answer with "Good morning," I respond by saying, "What do you mean, good morning? It's a great morning!" By the time the assistant stops laughing, I have that person onside and offering to help me.

Schmoozing a little bit goes a long way too. Whenever I need assistants to tell me the boss's availability, I'll use a line like, "Susan, since you are the keeper of John's calendar, you probably know more about John's life than he does. I was wondering if you could tell me when John is due back in?" I always get the information I need.

Whenever I'm speaking to the assistant for the second time in one day, having just missed my prospect and needing to find out for my Call Memo when the boss is due back in, a line like this never fails to get me the co-operation I need: "Joan! This is Steven Schwartz again. We have to stop meeting like this!" And they laugh every time.

You can also enhance your relationship with assistants by keeping them in the loop when you finally do book your appointment:

> *You:* Susan, thanks for putting me in touch with Steven. I spoke with him this morning and he booked an appointment for me to come in next Wednesday at 9:00. I will call you on Tuesday just to confirm.

The assistant will appreciate the feedback and the thanks, and will be all the more willing to help you confirm the appointment. By the way, before you go into your meeting, drop by the assistant's desk and thank the individual in person. That little personal touch will ensure that the assistant will continue to assist you throughout the sales cycle, especially when it comes to keeping you informed of any changes in the boss's schedule.

Here's an interesting remedy in the event that the

assistant (with the best of intentions) wants to pass your initial message along to the boss. This does not happen that often, but when it does I want you prepared and in complete control.

> *Assistant:* I'll pass that information along to Paul.
> *You:* Rather than take all your time writing this down, why don't I do you a favor Susan and send you the reason for my call in a few lines by e-mail. Would you like me to send it to your e-mail or directly to Paul's e-mail?(Wait for the answer and obtain the correct e-mail address.) Excellent. Could you do me a favor Susan; when you receive the message could you please print it out and place it on Paul's desk? Thanks a lot Susan!

You do not want the assistant to pass your message along verbally because quite often the integrity of the message never arrives intact. It can become a summary of what the assistant thought you said, rather than exactly what you said. Notice how you get around this by offering to do the assistant a favor by sending her the reason for your call. (You'll be sending her your script, beginning with the wording that comes after "I'm calling because.") When you do someone a favor they are likely to reciprocate. The favor in this case is having the assistant look out for your message, print it out, and then place it on the boss's desk. The fact that the assistant pulls your e-mail ensures that it does not get lost in the multitude of other messages. Printing it gives your message a physical presence, and makes it stand out. Having it placed on the boss's desk ensures that it gets seen, and is seen as something more urgent. If the boss is in at the time, the assistant has the opportunity to hand it over personally.

You probably observed one other powerful subtlety in

this method: Remember how you asked the assistant which e-mail address to send your message to? Other than the obvious need to know, the act of involving the assistant gives the individual some personal ownership over the message you are forwarding, since it is their choice where the message is to be sent. People support that which they help create.

Assistant Checklist

What doesn't work:
- ❏ Perceiving the assistant as an obstacle
- ❏ Being abrupt, forceful, and confrontational
- ❏ An impersonal approach

What does work:
- ❏ Perceiving the assistant as an ally
- ❏ The big schmooze
- ❏ First-name basis
- ❏ Positive attitude
- ❏ Sincerity
- ❏ Mentioning referrals
- ❏ Saying, "Good morning!" with enthusiasm
- ❏ Showing that you have something of value to offer
- ❏ Knowing something about the prospect/company
- ❏ Make 'em laugh and feel good
- ❏ Saying thank you
- ❏ A friendly call opens doors

Finally, make sure you stay in control of the conversation. Know when you want to speak to the assistant and for what purpose. Speak with the assistant to:

- ❏ Obtain the contact's direct line (if the receptionist doesn't know)
- ❏ Find out the best time to reach the assistant's boss (if the receptionist doesn't know)
- ❏ Confirm that the boss is in town

❏ *Inquire as to the best time to call back, when you miss the prospect (for your Call Memo)*

❏ *Note other comments about why the prospect is not in*

5. Voicefinder

A lot of people get hung up on what to say on someone's voicemail. Know what I say? Don't say anything. People tend to leave messages on voicemail as a crutch for not having to speak to prospects in person. They feel that by leaving a message either it's as good as speaking in person, which it's not, or the onus is now on the other person to call them back, which they won't. Even if someone does call you back, you will forfeit control. Do you remember the last time you left a message? When the person called you back a few days later you were multi-tasking ten issues, and on top of that you had completely forgotten about the call. When you picked up the phone and heard the prospect you said, "Who are you?" All your hard work down the drain. Never leave a message when you can speak in person. That's what Call Planning is about: getting a hold of people on the telephone to talk to them live. There is no substitute for it.

Voice mail is not without its merits. That's why I created VOICEFINDER. The idea is to access people's voice mail late in the evening, or early in the morning well before working hours so that you don't catch them in. (If you are calling a residence ask your phone company how to dial directly into someone's voicemail without having the phone ring on the other end.) I don't want you to talk. I want you to *listen*.

Listen to learn the correct pronunciation of the person's name. Listen to find out whether the person you want to reach is away from the office for an extended period of time. And since the first few seconds of your call are critical and you don't want to be taken by surprise, listen to familiarize yourself with the person's voice (do they sound harsh, or have a foreign accent?) and to determine the person's gender (is Pat, Chris, Michelle, or Jean male or female?). Keep this information on a pad near your phone. Recognizing the prospect's voice will also come in handy when the individual picks up the phone before the receptionist or assistant arrives. Since you won't have to ask who it is, your rapport will be enhanced by your ability to address the person without hesitation.

Finally, I want you to use voicemail as a motivational tool. Go back to when you and I were talking about overcoming the fear of technology, and I mentioned that you want to turn impersonal calls into personal calls (to compensate for the lack of body language). Voices are very personal, which makes them very powerful. They give you insights into personalities. It's amazing what you can discern about a person from a voice: whether the person is friendly, likes to get to the point, takes his or her time, or likes to go by a nickname. You can use this knowledge to adjust your tone and your pacing in the call once you open the conversation (but you must speak slowly in the first thirty seconds even if your prospect speaks quickly).

A voice message also creates an impression in your mind of what the person looks like. (If possible, see if you can view the prospect's picture on the company website.) That image will be more than enough to help personalize the call. Whatever image that voice on the other end conjures up, take a moment to reflect on it. That way, when you finally do speak in person, your familiarity with the person's voice will make you feel more at ease, more confident, and more focused on the call. (You'll learn more about how to use voicemail motivation in the Call Caffeine section's "Double Cream, All Sugar" technique.)

One last thought: While it's acceptable to leave a message once you have established a relationship, you should stay in the habit of speaking directly with your customers rather than playing telephone tag. There are two reasons for this. One is service. Not playing telephone tag is good customer service, plain and simple. If a customer calls you and leaves you a message, make every effort to reach them before they call you back again. If you get their voice-mail, leave a message only to inform them that you will call them later, so that they know you tried to reach them, and then call them back using the Call Planning methods you are now familiar with. (You may want to tell them when to expect your next call.)

Telephone tag is also the kiss of death for some deals because it causes precious momentum to be lost. The longer the space between calls, the greater the risk that the enthusiasm for the deal may cool. If you have to get back to someone with information, don't play tag. Play to win. Speak directly at all times to stay connected and ensure the deal is done.

6. Hot-Call Travel Planner

The last step of the call process deals with how to be prepared in advance for your out-of-town appointments. Has this ever happened to you? You call a company that is in another city, and just when you have the prospect agreeing to see you . . .

> *You:* When would be a good time to come in and see you?
>
> *Prospect:* This Wednesday at 10:00.
>
> *You:* Let me call you back after confirming the flight availability.

Two hours later, after you've checked the airlines for flights, you call back only to discover that your interested party is in a meeting; it takes you another two days to reach the person, by which time it's too late because it's Wednesday already. Or perhaps you did manage to get back to the person later that day, but by then you had given the individual time to reconsider having the meeting. Or perhaps the person was agreeable but, unfortunately for you, another commitment filled in your time slot just moments before you called back.

Take charge and stay in control. Do your homework in advance. Call your travel agent ahead of time and find out:

- Flight information (times, availability, and cost) for the month to allow for a large enough window of opportunity
- The distance and time from the airport to the prospect's office. That way you can predetermine how much time you'll need to get there if you're flying in just for the day, and will need to allow for the total time it will take to get to your appointment.

Having all the necessary information at your fingertips when you call allows you to strike while the commitment is hot. It makes you look like a seasoned professional who has travelled many times before and is always prepared. It also boosts your confidence — so critical to your success — because the process of checking with airlines and hotels lets you believe that the appointment is as good as booked. (Since the mental image you create is one of travelling to see your prospect, that's the action you will pursue.)

Being prepared pays off:

Prospect: How about tomorrow at 10:00?
    You: My flight arrives at 9:00, and I understand that you're at least 45 minutes from the airport — in good traffic — so to be safe, can we make it 11:00?
Prospect: (*Impressed*) You bet. Look forward to meeting you.

Your sales are due to take off any moment . . .

4

Strategic Scripting

*H*aving graduated from Call Planning with honors, you have every confidence that you will reach anyone, anytime. Yeah, even me. Well, it's a busy morning and, son of a gun, you nailed me just as I was coming into my office. Rrrrrrrrrring!

Me: Who can that be? Hello?
You: ?

Hey! That's your cue! Come on, this is your big moment. Now that you have me on the telephone, what do you want to say? More specifically, what could you possibly tell me that would pique my interest? What will you say that will make me want to listen to your every word, and then ask you to come in and see me? Talk to me. What do you have to offer?

And oh, by the way, we don't have time for small talk. No chit-chat and a walk over to the coffee room. You don't have the luxury of schmoozing on the telephone. Your message has to be direct and perfect, right from the start. Oh, I forgot, you have less than thirty seconds to get my interest. In fact, how well you come across in the *first few seconds* will set the stage for how receptive I am.

Might I suggest that now is a good time to learn how to write your telephone commercial? As in a radio commercial, every second counts and every single word is chosen to deliver results. Your opening line has to command attention and make someone want to listen to you and, ultimately, make an appointment to see you. It also has to create the right kind of impression so that you are taken seriously. Just as important, what you are about to learn moves you beyond obtaining a response to knowing how to control the precise response you just created.

One of the sacred cows of telemarketing is the assumption that prospects and customers want to hear from you, and that they will sit there passively and listen to what you have to say. Not true. People are busy. People don't jump out of bed waiting for your call (unless of course the taps are dripping again and you happen to be a plumber).

You have to make people listen, second by second, through the power of words and the passion with which they are spoken.

Here's another comparison to radio that's worth noting. In radio, every word paints an image in the mind of the listener, and the announcer has complete control over what those images are and the impact they will have. Radio is the most visual medium of all simply because the audience pictures the images in their own minds. Think about the last time you read a book and then later discovered that the movie version was less appealing. The images you created in your own mind with your own imagination were more powerful. When you speak on the phone, every word you utter will also paint an image in the minds of your prospects, and you will have complete control over what those images are. Control the images, control the outcome!

Think back to the last telephone sales call you made. Are you aware of what images you created in the mind of your prospect? Once you transmit an image you can't get it back; it's locked in your prospect's mind for years to come. Those images can either create the right set of expectations and shorten your sales cycle, or create the wrong impression and make it harder for you to establish a trusting relationship that will lead to positive results.

Here's a sobering thought: From the time you open your mouth to introduce yourself to the time you ask for the appointment, there are less than thirty words. That's right.

There are thirty words between you and every opportunity in the world.

These words are not arbitrary. They have meaning and they have impact. That's why this part of the system is dedicated to leveraging the power of words.

What would happen if you were in my office right now and I said, "You have thirty seconds to tell me why I should do business with you." What would you say? That's a serious question, because if it hasn't happened to you yet, it just might.

It happened to a graduate of York University named Zev who, as it turned out, read this book to help him land his first job. By applying the Call Planning methodology, Zev was able to reach the human resources decision-maker at a medical software company. Once he had the individual on the phone, Zev knew exactly what he needed to say to secure an interview, because he had applied the scripting process you are about to learn. Now here's the best part of the story. In the interview Zev was sitting there with the head of Human Resources, who told him point-blank, "You have one minute to tell us why we should hire you." Zev had done his homework by using the scripting tools to prepare an effective response to just such a question, which he delivered confidently and without hesitation. The HR person was so impressed (and surprised) that she hired Zev on the spot.

Now it's time to get you prepared to craft your own winning message. What I'm about to show you is a process for writing your telephone sales pitch as a telephone commercial. When you're finished, you will be able to answer that pointed question posed to Zev, in thirty seconds or less, either in person or over the telephone.

The process I'm going to share with you is called Strategic Scripting. It has the power not only to communicate what you're offering in a precise, convincing manner, but also to give you greater strategic insights into the products and services you offer.

Strategic Scripting is a framework for knitting together — word for word — your most persuasive opening line. As the name implies, Strategic Scripting is a carefully constructed sales patter that is based on a well-defined selling strategy. This is the same strategic thinking behind any other kind of commercial message that you would see on television, or hear on radio. The underlying idea is that before you develop your message, you must first define and then put into words exactly what you're selling or offering and why people would want to buy it, and then translate this selling concept into a strategy that will get people to listen to your message.

Let me give you an example. If I gave you a brochure, any brochure, why would you open it up? The odds are that you wouldn't. Why? Well, you're too busy, for one thing. For another, you get enough brochures shoved in your face every day. The truth is, most brochures don't give you cause to open them. There's no benefit statement (the reason why you would buy the product or service) on the cover. I've always told my clients that people don't want to read anything; you have to *make* them read your message. "In eight words or less," I used to say, "why would anyone want to open the brochure?" Anyone?

Try activating what I call the *greed glands* in people; they're tucked away somewhere in the back of the brain and light up every time someone hears something near and dear to their heart. Greed glands are triggered when the ears hear an answer to the question: "What's in it for me?" They come alive when people hear what they stand to gain. You can also stimulate the *fear glands* — the twin sister of greed glands — which work like raw nerves when there is talk about what people stand to lose. For example, if you were selling vitamins to give me more energy, that would appeal to my greed glands. If, on the other hand, you were selling vitamins to reduce my risk of catching the flu (and losing income as a result of it), you would be activating my fear glands.

At this point I want you to activate the greed glands by telling people in eight words or less on the cover of a brochure what it is they want to hear; what they're looking for, what they need etc. I never take my reader's attention for granted. I assume the worst (that the brochure will not be opened) and then make people listen to my message by giving them good reason to.

Just as you have to give people an incentive to open a brochure to read your message, you have to give people a reason to open up a dialogue to hear your message.

You haven't put your crayons away, have you? Good. Try this exercise. If you created a brochure to promote *you* as the product, what would you put on the cover — in eight words or less — to make someone open it up?

Now draw your cover.

```




```

Not easy, I know. Now ask yourself, "If someone called me on the telephone right now and told me those same eight words, would I want to listen?" *If you can't be sure that people would read your message, don't take it for granted that they would listen to it either.* Chances are they won't. And that's where you start. When you win over the worst cynics on their worst day, everyone and everything else will follow. Remember, go for the greed glands.

The process of creating compelling dialogue begins with the premise that you cannot take it for granted that anyone will listen. You have to give people a reason to listen. The goal is to have people listen to you not because they *have* to (because they don't), but because they *want* to.

Now before I continue, I'd better stop and make sure you're on board. There are lots of people who hear the word "script" and cringe. Unfortunately we've all been at the receiving end of telemarketers rambling on and on, reading from their scripts for what seems like an eternity before we can get a word in edgewise. That's not at all what I'm suggesting when we talk about scripts.

A script is simply dialogue. It's a way of introducing

yourself and the opportunity you'd love to share. *The call is only a conversation between two people.* Nothing more and nothing less. You are not going to be scripting the whole conversation. You will only need to prepare the first thirty seconds of it, in addition to the Objections Portfolio we discussed earlier. Within those thirty seconds you should be able to secure an appointment or sale, or at the very least obtain permission to talk in more detail, after which you can close successfully.

There is a myth out there that scripts by their very nature sound scripted, canned, and unnatural. Well, when you go to the theatre to see a play, the whole performance is scripted, and yet it doesn't sound like the actors are simply reading their lines. It sounds like they're having a normal conversation. So all you have to do is write your script conversationally and then deliver it conversationally. (We'll talk about delivery in the next section.)

A script creates a central theme going into the call that helps you focus on what you want to say.

It makes your message clear and meaningful to the listener, and gives your prospect a compelling reason to see you. Scripting your message also gives you consistency and predictability. A script that is created with attention to every word, and then is tested for effectiveness, enables you to take all the guesswork out of your success. Using a well-crafted script gives you confidence knowing that you will be successful time and time again. Without a script you are going in blind. A script also enables you to self-assess at the end of a call. (Remember, "Is it them or is it me?") If you keep changing the variables you will never know precisely where the problem is.

The whole exercise is simply to find the very words that will open the doors of opportunity for you, and then use them with confidence. Enough said. Let's continue with the scripting process.

Your call is divided into three parts:

A. *Reason for Call*
B. *Close*
C. *Recap*

Strategic Scripting helps you write and communicate part A. The Close deals with how you ask for the appointment, and the Recap summarizes important information once you get a firm commitment, which will happen as a result of the great job you did with A and B.

A. Reason for Call

This is the thirty-second script or dialogue I was talking about that gives the person you are calling both a reason to listen and an incentive to see you (or whatever your call objective might be, whether it's to get an appointment, to obtain information, or to make a sale). The process of mapping out your reason for calling is divided into two parts:

1. Finding the very words that will open the door of opportunity.
2. Blending them into a single, seamless thought.

The first part involves using a six-point strategic model, which is simply a series of six questions that you ask yourself and which, of course, you have to answer. (That's the challenge.) Here are the six questions:

Six-Point Strategic Model
   1. *What am I selling?*
   2. *To whom am I selling it?*
   3. *What do I want to say?*
   4. *What does my audience want to hear?*
   5. *What is my competition saying?*
   6. *What is my unique selling proposition?*

Answer each question on a separate page, either in complete sentences or in point form. Throw together any words or phrases that come to mind — don't worry about how it looks. You should end up with a large sheet of paper with a bunch of strategically defined words on it. From there you'll cull through the lot and begin creating a few sentences of dialogue that contain the strongest words, and then craft it so that the sentences form a grammatically correct, natural-sounding dialogue. It will all become clearer as we go through the exercise together. For now, take out a fresh sheet of paper and let's go through each question, one at a time. Take your time. While the questions are deceptively simple, the answers will require a lot of thought.

Throughout each exercise you'll see a section marked Personalized Answer #1, #2, and so on. That's where you should write down your answers to the questions in that exercise as it pertains *to your own business*. That way you will be able to take your answers and begin writing your opening line.

1. What am I selling?

Simple question, right? Not so fast. I don't want you to define what you are offering in terms of what your product or service is, but rather *why someone would buy it*. The question within the question to ask yourself is, "What am I *really* selling?" Come up with reasons that excite people. As advertisers say, don't think of the steak, give me the sizzle. The "steak" defines what you are offering in terms of what it is, and the "sizzle" defines your offering in terms of why someone would buy it.

Can You Find the Sizzle?

STEAK	SIZZLE
Refrigerator	_____
Home Repair	_____

Washing Machine _____

Shelving _____

Gardening Services _____

Lottery Ticket _____

Hey! Don't peek at the answers until you finish working them out for yourself. You're done? All right, here we go.

A refrigerator (that's the steak) is a product. Its sizzle is why you buy it: for food preservation. The better the refrigerator, the better your food is preserved. That's why I think that if you were selling refrigerators, you would have more success uttering the words "food preservation" somewhere in your opening line or two.

Home repair is a service. But what are you really looking for in a home repair person? My experience, like most people's, is that while all home repair people do repairs, what I'm really looking for when something needs fixing is someone who is going to come and fix it *right away*. What I really want then is reliability. I want to know that the person will actually show up on time. Hey, if you're a handy person, I wouldn't stress home repair, but rather reliability. That's what people are really buying.

A washing machine is, well, a washing machine. What are you *really* buying? Fabric care. You don't want something that just gets your clothes clean. You want your good clothes to come out of the wash in one piece and last a long time. You're talking about cleanliness and protecting your investment in your clothing.

Now shelving. Well, I don't know about you but I didn't wake up this morning saying, "Hey, I need shelving." But everyone on the planet can sure use more space. If you were in the shelving business, do you think you'd sell more shelves by referring to yourself as a space saver? (Hear the sizzle?) Tell me, do you need shelving, or would you like to talk about how I can get you more space?

Last week I got a call from a gardener asking if I'd be interested in fertilizing and weed control and every other gardening service he could list. When the neighbors walk by my house to admire the garden, it's not the grass seed I'm showing off. It's the lush green lawn.

Finally, don't forget to buy a lottery ticket this week, and when you do, you won't be buying a ticket, you'll be buying (help me out here) . . . that's it — you'll be buying a dream!

Getting to the sizzle is a continuous process of digging around until you get to the bottom of the answer. You are constantly asking questions within your questions. Let's get you more familiar with the technique.

Imagine if you will, that you are responsible for marketing a leading Canadian newspaper. In a drive for subscriptions, you organize a telemarketing campaign; in other words, you're going to call up prospective customers to sell them subscriptions.

What is the steak?

_____

(Answer: Subscriptions)

What is the sizzle?

_____
_____
_____

(Answer: Good question. So let's get out of these brackets and continue . . .)

This exercise was inspired after I received an uninspired call one day from a leading newspaper. "We're calling today, Mr. Schwartz, to offer you a subscription . . ." Stop right there. I don't need a subscription. See the problem? I was eating vegetarian that day; I wasn't in the market for steak. Now, if they gave me the sizzle, I would bite.

Once again, what is the sizzle? Let's listen for it . . . Can't hear it yet, so here goes. What are they really selling?

Try information.

Everyone wants information. We all live in an information economy, and since every person in business needs information to succeed, the next logical question to ask would be, "What kind of information?" This isn't a magazine that comes out once a month. It's a newspaper you get every day. That makes it . . .

timely information

So far, so good. Keep digging. Let's go back to our steak. A subscription is nothing more than a convenience, because the newspaper is delivered to your door. Ahhhh! In other words, the information comes to me. So the real service being provided is . . .

access to timely information

I would have been a lot more interested in listening to what the salesperson was talking about if they had told me right up front, "Mr. Schwartz, I'm calling to offer you access to timely information." My gut response would have been to ask, "What kind of information?" See what happened: they hit my greed glands! They said something of interest I wanted to hear and, as a result, it made me open up a dialogue.

In the previous example, "access to timely information" would be what I call a generic sizzle, since it is not specific to any one audience. It's a good place to begin before you customize your sizzle further. We will move on to that shortly because the more specific your audience, the more specific your sizzle and your message need to be.

Now, a lot of people mistake their products and services for the sizzle since they sound exciting to the people who sell them. They don't necessarily sound exciting to the people they are selling them to. A product or a service are "steaks" since they define your offering in terms of what it is. No one wakes up in the morning thinking about your product, unless it's coffee. That's one reason why your products and services should not be mentioned in the first thirty seconds. The other reason is because products and services are only a means to an end. If the end is not articulated and agreed to, you will sound like you're selling instead of sharing an opportunity. How many times has someone called you up and said, "I'd like to come and see you to talk about our new such-and-such product." Don't they sound like they're just pushing the product of the week on you? So please make sure that words like "product," "service," "program," "promotion," or "solution" do not appear within the first thirty seconds of your call.

Suppose you were selling high-resolution computer monitors that reduced eye strain. If you called someone up and asked them if they'd like to buy a high-resolution monitor (the steak), they'd more than likely say no unless they needed one that day. You'd also sound like you're selling something. However, if you called to say that you can increase the length of time they spend on the computer by reducing eye strain (the sizzle), you would not only have the person's attention, but also sound like you are offering an opportunity to fill a need. If the person says that they'd like to know how you make that possible, you would then proceed to tell them about the monitor, which as you know is only a means to the end you just articulated.

Now it's time to look at your own product or service and get your sizzle going. Sssssssssssssssss.

Your steak:

_____

Personalized answer #1 (your generic sizzle):

_____

_____

A surefire way to test the impact of your sizzle is to answer the following question:

Do your prospects wake up in the morning saying, "I need . . . "?

_____

_____

(Fill in your sizzle)

If the answer is no, you need to more sharply define and articulate how you can help your audience solve their top issues, and how your offerings appeal to the audience mind-set. Here's a general tip for any audience: People wake up with needs, problems, wants, and desires.

2. To whom am I selling it?

Your sizzle will need to be modified to reflect the unique issues and mind-set of your audience. That's why if you are calling on several different audiences, each will need it's own script. How often has some telemarketer called you up and left you asking the question, "Why are they calling *me*?" That happens whenever their message does not really apply to your circumstance. By asking the question, "To whom am I selling?" you force yourself to address the unique and individual mind-set of your audience. If you are calling up every business in the book, you are addressing a general audience. A general audience gets a general message.

However, if you are addressing a specific audience, that is to say a specific industry segment (transportation, insurance, retail, industrial, pharmaceutical, financial, etc.) or business segment (small business vs. large corporation) or audience type (VP level vs. CEO), then you are addressing a vertical audience, which means you must have a vertical message. (A vertical message addresses the particular issues, language, cultures, and needs of a very specific target audience.) The more targeted your audience, and the more specifically your message is tailored to your audience, the higher your results will be.

General audience ☛ *General message*
Vertical audience ☛ *Vertical message*

Let's go back to our previous newspaper example. If you were selling access to timely information, that would suffice for a general audience. However, suppose you were going to target your calls to very *specific* groups of people: those who read the sports section, those who peruse the travel section, readers who browse through the classifieds, and entrepreneurs who devour the business section. Each group would be a vertical market. To be as effective at reaching these different groups as possible, your message will have to be as specific as possible, addressing the unique needs of each target audience.

The kind of timely information people would access would depend on which vertical audience you're targeting. It might be:

- Access to timely business information
- Access to timely market updates
- Access to timely job leads
- Access to timely vacation deals
- Access to timely sports scoops

You get the idea. Let's take a moment and define your audience. First, let's see how vertical you want to go. Each vertical level will have different issues you will need to address. For example, if you are targeting the transportation industry, your audience will have different issues than say, the financial industry. On the next level you will notice that the size of the company adds a new layer of complexity because a small transportation company will have different issues and needs than a large one. At the next level you will observe that a CEO of a transportation company will have different issues depending on the size of the organization; a start-up company may be consumed with cash flow and a mature company concerned with market share, growth, and acquisitions. A CEO of such a company will also have different issues than those in the purchasing department; the CEO might be looking to acquire the latest technology while the purchasing manager is only interested in buying technology at the lowest cost. Location too has a role in shaping your audience; a company on the West Coast may have different needs compared to those on the East Coast (environmental issues, transportation costs, access to local or foreign markets etc.).

You can also modify the way you segment your vertical markets by targeting individuals rather than organizations. For example, retirees can be segmented into various groups, including people who are about to retire, those just retired, and those who have been retired for many years. Each level will have distinct issues to address. Furthermore, this group can be further segmented into disposable income levels and locations (rural vs. urban, regional access to medical facilities and lower cost medications etc.).

So, what's your audience look like?

Personalized answer #2 (your vertical audience):

Industry segment: _____

Size of company/purchases: _____

Job Title (CEO, CFO, Self-Employed, etc.): _____

Type of customer: _____

Customer's income/net worth: _____

Customer's status: _____

Location: _____

Now that you know who you are marketing to, let's identify the specific needs of that audience. For example, a CEO might be concerned with shrinking margins. A

Chief Financial Officer (CFO) might need better control over expenses or more timely, accurate reporting. Lawyers want to get paid right away. Oil and gas companies are concerned with security in remote locations. Mining companies need money for exploration. (I could go on and on.)

Personalized answer #3 (the top three issues your audience is concerned with):

1. _____
2. _____
3. _____

Next, let's move on to the unique mind-set of your audience. Mind-set differs from issues as it deals with how people think or feel. For example, customers can be told that there are better deals out there, yet they will still be cynical because they don't believe they are actually getting them. So when speaking to that mind-set you would do well to quantify the savings or potential savings you are presenting.

CFOs live in a world of details, facts and figures. Once again, you will win points when you properly address that mind-set. How? By being very specific and backing up your statements with hard numbers and facts whenever possible.

When selling to someone who is extremely cost sensitive, words like "low cost," "value," and "deals" are effective in awakening the greed glands.

If you're offering something that is in any way technical, you may find yourself faced with an audience that is confused. A phrase like, "I will walk you through..." will put them at ease, as will any reference to "clarity" or "simplicity."

Should you find yourself calling on someone with an analytical mind-set, remember that analytical people love details; if you have a process, call it a "detailed process" and you'll have their undivided attention. If the individual is a Type A personality who likes to get to the point quickly, the word "brief" registers nicely.

Personalized answer #4 (the mind-set of your audience):

1. _____
2. _____
3. _____

At this point you have successfully identified your audience(s) and the associated issues and mind-set. Let's use that information to adjust your sizzle to reflect those needs and that mind-set. Here's an example. Suppose you worked for a railroad company and one of your vertical markets was plastics manufacturers.

> *Issue:* In order to stay competitive they must have access to low-cost resins (the material plastic is made of).
>
> *Mind-set:* Worried about maintaining a reliable supply of resins.
>
> *Sizzle:* Access to lower cost suppliers. A secure supply of resins.

Whenever you apply that sizzle you will know that you are either touching on the greed glands (access to low-cost resins) or the fear glands (secure supply of resins). When you mention low-cost resins, the customer envisions dollar signs. When you mention a secure supply of resins to your audience, that worried feeling creeps in as that person begins to wonder if the current supply is going to run out any minute, causing the plant to grind to a very expensive halt.

You could easily apply both sizzles in your script, face-to-face meetings, presentations and proposals; as you do this you will quietly control what your audience is thinking and feeling (a.k.a. greed/fear glands). Just for fun, here are two applications where you can apply your sizzle.

Telephone Sales Call Script

> *"Good morning Mr. Donohue. We haven't been introduced before, my name is Steven Schwartz from ABC Railroad Company. And I'm calling because we've been very successful in helping plastics manufacturers access lower cost suppliers, and we do that Mr. Donohue through our network of vendors who guarantee a secure supply."*

Networking

If you were asked at a party what you do at the railroad company, your sizzle would create an enticing answer, which could be as simple as, "I help plastics manufacturers pay less for resins and make sure they never run out."

Personalized answer #5 (adjust your sizzle to address the issues and mind-set of your audience): Select one audience for now.

_____

_____

_____

3. What do I want to say?

In the old paradigm, what you want to say is an important part of your message. In this new paradigm, what you want to say is the least important part of the opening dialogue. The emphasis is on your audience, not you. This is not to say that benefit statements do not have their place. They do, only if they tickle the greed glands. If not, leave them out of your telephone commercial, and introduce them after you open up the conversation, or in your future conversations with that prospect.

At this point I need you to list your number one benefit, because that's all you'll have time for within a thirty second window. Don't confuse benefits with features. If you are selling cars, the tinted windows and sports wheels are features. The benefit is the associated prestige. Now think about your offering: Do you help people save time/money, achieve goals, feel better etc.?

Personalized answer #6 (main benefit):

_____

_____

4. What does my audience want to hear?

Suppose you and I are smack in the middle of playing a game of chess. You're black, I'm white. Now move the board around and switch. You're playing with the white players and I'm using black. Suddenly the game takes on a new perspective, and you're seeing the board from my point of view. With that perspective in mind, let's get back to your Strategic Scripting. Look at your message from the other side. Forget what you want to say for a moment. What does your audience want to hear? It can be something completely different than what you want to say.

This is a powerful part of your message. When people hear words that they want to hear, their greed glands go hyperactive. Why? Simply because people act on *their* needs, not yours. When you know specific words people want to hear, use them in your telephone sales call, face-to-face meetings and proposals. Whatever words they want to hear must be said in a language people understand and can relate to.

People must understand and relate to what you
are saying before they will take action.

Most industries and organizations have their own internal language with its own terminology and buzz words. But when you use such language with an audience from another company or industry, people often don't understand or relate to what you're saying (and they may be too polite to tell you that they don't know what you're talking about). What's important is that you speak their language, not yours. For example, if you are calling on people in the recording industry, one word instantly comes to mind: Collaborate. Recording is all about collaboration. So, if you begin your call by saying "I collaborate with recording executives to...," you instantly send a message that you are one of them, or at the very least you understand their industry. People can relate to the word collaborate, and in doing so, your audience will instantly relate to you.

Personalized answer #7 (industry/corporate jargon):

_____

People also want to hear how you can help them solve their problems. As I mentioned before, people don't want to hear about products right away. Address their issues, not yours. For example, as a financial consultant dealing with retirees, you should know that these people are very concerned with protecting themselves against the rising cost of living. Talk about this issue and they'll be all ears. Know what problems your audience is facing. If you don't have specific solutions to specific problems, find them; or better yet, invent them — you'll be a hero, and probably make a fortune!

Often people will tell you what they need in order for them to make a purchase. You might know this information as "deal makers." Have you ever had someone tell you, "What I'm looking for is a way to . . ." or, "What I'm looking for is someone to help me . . . " or, "If you can get me . . . I'll buy it from you . . ." ? Whatever they use to fill in the blanks will give you insight into the very words they want to hear from you. For example, if lots of people keep telling you that they want a product just like yours, but without paying for a minimum volume, then you just learned that whenever you mention "no minimum volume," you will activate the greed glands.

Personalized answer #8 (your top three deal makers):

1. _____
2. _____
3. _____

Of course, people are always telling you what's important to them, but it's up to you to really listen closely to what they are saying. Here's a great story to illustrate the point. I received a call one day from a derivatives dealer at a large Wall Street firm, asking for help in preparing for a meeting they were having with a VP at a telecommunications company. The deal was in the tens of millions of dollars, so they wanted to make sure they walked in ready to hit a home run. It turns out that this financial institution had been the first to notice that the telecommunications company was overexposed to currency fluctuations because of a large European presence.

In a conference call I asked the individual and his colleagues to tell me what sort of conversations they had been having from the time they established contact with this company some months ago. All I was listening for was a word or phrase that would repeat itself. During an hour on the phone, I noticed that one word had in fact come up in almost every conversation they were discussing. It was the word "simple." I told my client that "simple" was important to this telecommunications VP, and that they had better use it in the first thirty seconds when they opened the meeting. We then proceeded to use this six-point model to create the opening line, which went like this: "We have invested the time to structure a simple strategy that will reduce the volatility in your earnings." I told my client to watch for a change in the VP's body language when the word "simple" came up.

After the meeting I got a call from my client. As it turned out, after they sat down and said their lines, guess what happened? The VP moved her chair in, leaned across the desk, and said, "Simple is exactly what I need to take to the board." My client could not believe their "luck," and their proposal was soon on the way to the board. But luck had no part in it. Anyone can knock the eight ball into the side pocket, but it's another thing altogether to call it in advance. We knew the one word that the VP wanted to hear, and we played that shot with confidence.

In the future, keep track of words or expressions that surface in every conversation. These don't just have to be words that your customers use. They might be words you use unknowingly that somehow pique people's interest. Make a mental note every time that happens; sure enough, you will see a pattern developing where the same words or thoughts surface time and again. These words are gold.

Personalized answer #9 (what you said in the past that immediately captured the interest of your prospects):

_____

_____

_____

_____

_____

Personalized answer #10 (words your audience want to hear):

_____

_____

_____

5. What is my competition saying?

One very good reason why someone will want to do business with you is because you are offering something better than your competition does. You can't afford to come across as just another "me too" offering. Do some research and find out what your competition is saying about:

- Their products and services
- Their company in general

- The image they are portraying
- Specific promises or claims
- Timely offers
- Your company
- You!

Look through your competitors' advertising, or call them directly yourself, posing as a customer requesting some sales literature. Other sources of information would include trade shows, advertising, direct marketing, telemarketing, the Internet, newsletters, industry reports/journals, colleagues, and even asking *your* customers what they think and know about the competition.

Respond to your competitor's strengths (match offers, price, etc.). Exploit their weaknesses. If your competition can't guarantee twenty-four-hour delivery and you can, make a point of bringing that out in your conversation (without specifically mentioning your competitor by name). Sometimes this information will not be used in your script, but it will be invaluable when compiling your objection responses.

Personalized answer #11 (your competition's number one strength and how you can respond to it, plus, the main competitive weakness and how you can exploit it):

_____

_____

_____

_____

_____

_____

6. What is my unique selling proposition?

If you can provide a value-added solution that the competition can't, say it! Whenever you can say something that the competition can't, that is called a unique selling proposition. Ask yourself, "What do I have that my prospects want, which my competitors can't deliver? What is the added value I bring to the table that the competition doesn't?" Your unique selling proposition will be either *what* you offer or *how* you offer it. Whenever you can offer something that the competition cannot, exploit that strength by communicating your unique selling proposition. But make sure it is truly unique. If you don't have a unique selling proposition, *create one.*

If you feel that you are too close to be objective, conduct an informal customer survey. Over lunches or coffee casually ask a dozen of your good customers, "Why are you happy doing business with me?" Then stop talking and listen very carefully to what they say. Very often your customers know more about what is unique about your business than you do. If many of the customers you ask point to the same thing, this indicates that something unique may be there. I collected all my unique selling propositions from either asking my clients directly, or listening to exactly what they said when they paid a compliment.

If your unique selling proposition does not seem to work into your script for whatever reason, you can use this information right away in your objection responses.

Personalized answer #12 (what you can say that your competitors can't):

_____

_____

_____

At the beginning of this section I mentioned that there are two parts in the process of mapping out your reason for calling. You have just completed the first part, which involved finding the words that will open doors for you. Revisit your "personalized answers" and underline the words and thoughts that are most interesting or relevant. Those will now form the basis of your script. (Write them down on a fresh sheet of paper.) The second part of the process involves taking those thoughts and blending them into a single, conversational phrase; this will form the first thirty seconds of your script.

On a fresh sheet of paper, write down the following:

"Good morning (name of prospect). We've never been introduced before; my name is (your name) from (name of your company). And I'm calling because..."

That opening phrase never changes. It's the thirty words that follow that you now need to craft.

Six steps are required to accomplish this.

1. Place your sizzle and words your audience want to hear within the first fifteen words. It's the best way to get immediate attention.

2. Do a word count from after "And I'm calling because . . ." to just before you ask for the appointment. There should be no more than thirty words in a single sentence. I'm a bit fussy about this "single sentence" business because I've noticed that whenever I get a call from someone who sounds like they are talking to a machine instead of to me, it's often because they're talking on and on in many sentences, and as a result, end up sounding like they are talking to themselves. So please keep it to one sentence, with a comma in the middle if need be.

3. Review every single word to make sure each one creates a strong image, and that it's the image you want projected. Wherever possible use adjectives/adverbs to describe key words.

As I've mentioned earlier, every word you speak paints an image in the mind of the person you are calling, and you have complete control over what those images are. People move in the direction of the images they create or the ones you create for them. That means that you can change one word and change the outcome simply by making that image more interesting, visual, or memorable. I'll give you an example. What comes to mind when I say "small business?" (Take a moment and ponder.) What comes to mind when I say "local business?" What comes to mind when I say "independent business?" What comes to mind when I say "established business?" All I did was change one word and yet I managed to change the image in your mind.

Last month one of the account managers I was coaching at Canadian National Railway was calling on shippers and we were playing with the word "shipment." Eventually we substituted "inventory" for "shipment" to make our message more compelling to the shipper. Here's why. To a shipper a shipment is "stuff in a box going out" while inventory creates an image of "stuff on the floor I have to deal with." If you have to deal with it you don't want any screw-ups, hence there was a more emotional tie-in with the message.

Now that you've seen how a single word can change the outcome, let's go to the next step and add some descriptive words. When you make a word more descriptive you create a more interesting visual in your listener's mind. You also make your conversation more meaningful. Suppose you said, "I specialize in offering advice to executives who are planning for retirement." Watch how you can change the images in your mind by making the words more descriptive:

"I specialize in offering (proven) advice to executives who are planning for (an early/a carefree/an unforeseen) retirement."

In the above example, when you say you have proven advice, you create a specific set of expectations. Notice how an early retirement activates the greed glands, a carefree retirement connects more with your emotions, and an unforeseen retirement touches the fear glands.

You would need to make a decision on which image is more appropriate, and if need be, test them to find out. There are all kinds of options you will have to consider when choosing your words. Don't make every word descriptive for its own sake. Be selective, and be aware that you have control over the images you are putting out there.

4. Prioritize your words to make sure your prospect is motivated to listen second by second. Like radio, your telephone commercial has to make people listen every step of the way. Never assume someone is listening. Make them listen. Divide your message into short segments and then ask yourself, if you were the prospect, would you continue to listen for another few seconds? If the answer is no, stop right there and adjust that segment until the answer is yes. (You may need to rearrange or replace some words.)

   Here's a short, simple example:

   "I'm calling because we help furniture manufacturers / grow revenues / by giving them access / to markets they couldn't reach before."

   In the first segment I've identified the audience I'm speaking with, so at the very least they know that I understand their business. It also tells them that I have worked with their competitors. In the second segment the greed glands should perk up at the sound of the sizzle, since there isn't a furniture manufacturer on this planet who would not want to grow revenues. In the third segment I've piqued their interest because they're wondering "access to what?" In the final segment I have zeroed in on an issue they are dealing with (in this case, opening up new markets).

5. Eliminate any negative words. Negative words paint negative images. If you deliver packages "damage free" your prospect might only hear "damage." In that example

you might want to say that you deliver packages safely to their destination.

6. Your dialogue must sound natural and totally conversational. This is the most challenging part, since people have a tendency to sound formal when they're writing. If need be, after you have gone through the previous five steps, put your pen down or walk away from the keyboard, and just talk the talk. Then write down what you just said. Play it into your voicemail and then take a five-minute break. When you go back to listen to your voice message, your script should sound as natural as if someone was standing there talking with you.

Here are three examples of how simple and conversational a script should be.

"I'm calling because I've been very successful in protecting retirees from the rising cost of living, and I do that Steven by making sure that the money they've saved is actually invested safely."

"I'm calling because I can help you to dramatically lower the daily energy expenses in your manufacturing, and avoid overspending, simply by using our purchasing power to negotiate better deals on your behalf."

"I'm calling because a lot of chemical distributors rely on us to improve their product margins by connecting them with lower-cost suppliers."

Notice how simple and conversational a good script can be. As easy going as the word arrangements sound, what is different with this approach is that you are now aware of the images you are creating in the minds of your listeners, and by doing so, controlling the way the listener will react. Your images are tailored to the unique mind-set and issues of your audience, using words your audience want to hear, and causing the greed glands or fear glands to tingle. By doing this, you create and precisely control the response you want.

Let's put your newfound knowledge to the test. Take a moment and put on your Hot Calls 3-D glasses and tell me what you see when you look at the following script. (The target audience is Chief Financial Officers.)

"We can save up to thirty per cent[1] on your business expenses next quarter[2], and the best part Steven is that you[3] can verify[4] those savings every month[5] with very accurate[6] reporting[7] that we supply you with."

1. This appeals to the mind-set of the audience since CFOs love facts and figures. Chances are the prospect is skeptical of such a claim unless it can be substantiated. Greed glands have kicked in.
2. Fear glands have surfaced since the CFO is picturing all the expenses that are piling up. A sense of urgency is beginning since the expenses have to be covered next quarter.
3. Credibility is created because the prospect does the verifying.
4. The skepticism has been removed by the word verify, since it looks like the claim of thirty per cent savings can be substantiated after all. Curiosity is taking over as the prospect is wondering exactly how they will verify the savings.(Hold that thought.)
5. Added credibility since these savings are verified every month. Curiosity is building around how the savings are actually verified.
6. Added credibility with the accuracy. This is also a word CFOs want to hear.
7. Curiosity over verifying the savings is satisfied. Greed glands and fear glands are stimulated simultaneously. Reports appeal to CFOs' greed glands because they love reports. On the other hand, if it's a report they are not

aware of, or do not have and should, then the fear glands take over.

It's amazing what those Hot Calls 3-D glasses will uncover. There is no guesswork as to what is going on in the mind of the listener. However, the best is yet to come. In the previous script, you can be fairly certain that your remark will cause a prospective CFO to ask you about the reporting, and you will be ready with an excellent answer. Now that's what I call the ultimate in control!

B. The Close

Having properly introduced yourself and given the prospect a reason to listen to you, now what? As they say in sales, you have to ask for the order! At the conclusion of your call, ask for whatever it is you want to accomplish. (Make sure you are clear on what your call objective is *before* you call.) Are you calling to:

- Book an appointment?
- Obtain/send information?
- Make a sale?

What is your call objective?

_____

Why is this your call objective?

_____

After stating your reason for calling, make your close. Since you have already activated the greed glands, closing should be as light as a feather. If you have a qualifying question to ask ahead of your close, keep in mind that by first stimulating the greed glands you have increased the desire of your audience to open up a conversation with you.

Here are a few examples of conversational ways to ask for the appointment:

"I was wondering, if at any point, you'd be interested in getting together to discuss..."
"When can we meet to discuss this further?"
"I'd appreciate the opportunity to meet to..."

Nothing hard sell about it. Gentle and assumptive is all you need once you activate greed glands to pique interest.

In the event you go for your close and do not get a "yes" right away, be prepared with a convincing reply. The person will either have a legitimate concern to express, a point that needs further clarification, or he or she may simply not be interested at this time. Anticipate what might be asked so you remain in control.

An effective response prepared ahead of time will tilt the odds of success in your favor. Make sure you speak slowly when answering questions or replying to an objection; speaking quickly makes you sound defensive while speaking slowly sends a message that you are supremely confident.

C. Recap

Once your call objective has been met (i.e., your appointment has been booked), confirm the details of your meeting:

- Repeat the time and place of your meeting. Call the receptionist back for the correct address and directions. (This way you don't take up any more of the person's valuable time.) If you're calling a residence, use a map to get directions.
- Always say thank you and especially thank people for their time.

"I'd just like to confirm that we'll be meeting at 127 Winding Blvd. at 10:00 a.m., Thursday, March 15. Is that correct? Thank you for your time, and I look forward to meeting you, Mrs. Smith."

Afterthought

Now that you know how to compose a convincing message and activate the old greed glands, it's time to revisit the finer subtleties of the script that are at play here. A short while ago I asked you to write the following:

"Good morning (name of prospect). We've never been introduced before; my name is (your name) from (name of your company). And I'm calling because . . ."

Let's take a closer look at this structure.

"Good morning (name of prospect) . . ."

Notice that I didn't ask "How are you?" That remark is what I refer to as a trip wire, because you can sabotage your whole success right there in the first few seconds without even knowing what hit you. Since people know you don't really mean it, you risk coming across as insincere. Even worse, the person may think for a moment that you are an acquaintance, and when they discover that you are not, they will feel cheated. Say good morning (or good afternoon) only, but with enthusiasm and energy. Sound like you mean it. Should someone say good morning back to you, don't say "How are you?" Instead say, "It's a great morning!" with a lot of enthusiasm. It will be contagious!

Another classic trip wire is when you ask, "Is now a good time to talk?" Why would it be? You called unannounced while someone was in the middle of a hundred different things. Right there people more often than not will answer no, and then where does that leave you? I know that it's a very respectful thing to ask, and I was raised to be respectful, but asking "Is now a good time to talk" in this environment does not work in your favor. What is different in this system is that once you hit the greed glands, people will find the time to listen. If they are genuinely busy, but liked what they heard, they will ask you to call them back later that afternoon.

A third trip wire to avoid occurs when calling a residential number. I can't tell you the number of times someone has called me at home and said, "Is Mr. or Mrs. Schwartz in?" How impersonal! They sound like they don't even know who they want to talk to. If you are calling Mr. Schwartz and a man answers, just assume that the person is Mr. Schwartz. If the gentleman is not Mr. Schwartz, he'll tell you. If he is Mr. Schwartz, you will have begun your conversation with confidence, and will have established a friendly rapport right off the bat.

"We've never been introduced before . . ."

This line is subtle yet powerful. It's your verbal handshake. Rather than come on strong and say, "This is Steven Schwartz calling," stop and think what that means to the person I am calling. Since I have called unannounced, does the person really care who I am? Unless my company name is well known and respected, that too means very little (other than the value of knowing to whom you are speaking). There is something presumptuous and arrogant about coming on and saying who you are, with the assumption that you are important to anyone other than yourself. "We've never been introduced before," is a humble preamble to your name, and it does not assume that you are the center of the universe. It does, however, earn you the right to announce who you are and, in a clever way, implies that an introduction is in order. Besides, introductions are always an appropriate way to meet someone.

". . . my name is (your name) . . ."

Your name is going to be important to your customer one day, since you're going to be doing business together very soon. Say your name slowly so that you get heard and taken seriously.

". . . from (name of your company) . . ."

Say your company name with pride and enthusiasm. If *you* don't like your company, why should the person you are calling? Sound happy and others will listen.

"And I'm calling because . . ."

This establishes the fact that there really is a reason for the call. If you were the listener, you would want to know right away that this call is about something of interest, and not a waste of time. Therefore, "I'm calling because," is another way of saying to the prospect, "There is a good reason for calling and could you hold on one more second and hear what it is?" Many people announce themselves and then rush in with, "We have a special this week" or "We sell carpet cleaning" or whatever, but I find it helpful to earn the right to mention your offer by implying that your offer is of value. It whets the appetite a little, and keeps people listening. You might argue that taking an extra second here is a second too much, but I've never had people hang up on me here. On the contrary, they listen.

This is no coincidence. Those three little words, when you say them right, are probably the most intimate moment in the conversation. Here's what I mean: If I were in your office for the first time and I said, "I'm here today because," I would be leaning across the desk looking you in the eyes. When I'm on the phone and I slowly say, "I'm calling because," I am leaning into the phone as I picture myself leaning across your desk. I'm so connected with you at that moment that it sounds like I'm right there across your desk giving you my undivided attention.

There is one instance when you need to replace "I'm calling because" and that's when you have a referral. I like to say, "Good morning. We've never been introduced before. My name is Steven Schwartz and I was referred to you by Doris Fulton. Doris urged me to call you because . . ." Notice the image I created around Doris. She was so excited about what I had to offer her associate that she didn't just ask me to call, she *urged* me to call. Subtleties are everything when you want to capture attention.

And while I have *your* attention a moment longer, I'd also like to express my views on the practice of sending letters before you call, and then referring to your letter in your opening remark. Letters are terrific door openers. In direct marketing, it has been proven that telemarketing campaigns are always more effective when preceded by a letter campaign that introduces the company and the call that is about to follow. Don't feel you have to write a letter, but if you do, I would like to offer a word of caution about referring to your letter in the conversation.

I take a somewhat contrary position. I feel that you should not mention your letter when you call. Now, now, I can see your eyebrows rising. Before you say anything, hear me out. (I had the same reaction from clients before I proved in their telemarketing campaigns that my strategy outperformed conventional wisdom.)

There are three scenarios that will occur when someone receives your letter.

1. *The individual has not had time to open your letter.*
2. *The person has read your letter and, while they love what you have to offer, they simply haven't had time to call you.*
3. *The reader doesn't like your offer. Full stop.*

Now let's review these three scenarios closely:

1. Since the individual hasn't read your letter, they will ask you what it said, obliging you to ramble on about its contents. Since the first thirty seconds is the most critical to your success, you don't want to waste your best shot speaking in the past tense. Concentrate on the present tense. Go back to the idea that this is a telephone commercial. You don't hear radio commercials begin with, "This is how we first wrote this script"; you hear the radio commercial. That's why you should just dive right into your telephone commercial and give the person the best reason to see you.

2. In this scenario, the person likes what you have to offer and will welcome a call from you. But let's go back to basic psychology for a moment. Ask yourself, "Which is more powerful, talking about your letter to someone who has already read it, or not mentioning the letter, thereby triggering the other person's memory so that they go deep into their own minds (unprompted) and recall your letter all by themselves?" Well? It's a thousand times more powerful when someone uses their own energy and concentration to recall your letter because, at that point, they are highly focused on your letter. In the process, I might add, they are reliving positive emotions, reflecting on something they liked, which works very well in your favor.

3. And now for the reader who has read your letter and doesn't like your offer. Why flog a dead horse? That person is recalling negative emotions, and you will have an uphill battle from then on. Better that you should start fresh and open with your dynamic telephone commercial with a convincing thirty-second patter. Create positive feelings, and change the person's mind!

I hope you take my advice. If you like, test it out. If you are inclined to send letters out before you call, make ten calls referring to your letter and ten not referring to your letter, and see which approach works best. I believe you will find my observation to be correct.

One final point on scripting. The whole point of the exercise is to find the very words that will open the door of opportunity. Feel free to make two or three versions of your script, and test them to ascertain which one works best for you (run each script through at least twenty calls). *Once you have a script that is a winner, don't change it.* I can't tell you how many times people create a perfectly successful telephone commercial and then change it. Why do they do that? They're bored! Well, the way I see it, you're in the business of making successful telephone sales calls, and that's what you should stick to. When you have something that works, why on earth would you resort to potluck? Simply knowing that something works builds confidence, and confidence comes across loud and clear on the other end of the telephone and gets you in the door.

If your problem is boredom, handle the boredom but leave your script intact. *Have a break. Don't break your success.* Take longer breaks, go for walks, read a magazine. If you want variety, think about all the different things you will be able to buy and all the places you will be able to travel to once those calls generate appointments and sales. Focus on success.

I'm focused on your success.
Stay with me.

5

Script Delivery

*W*hat does a telephone sales call have in common with a Shakespearean play? Delivery. The story you are telling is only as good as the people telling it. Powerful words are not enough. The delivery — the way you say those words — can make or break your production. This is one of the reasons why a telephone sales call is like a radio commercial. Why do you suppose radio commercial producers go to great lengths to work with their actors to get the "perfect read"? And what do they do at that point? They record it, and that's what you end up hearing on the radio. You not only hear the perfect read, you hear it every time. That's what you have to do with your telephone commercial. You need to deliver your strategic script in as natural and convincing a manner as possible, and be able to deliver this perfect read every time.

The good news is that you are about to learn several innovative techniques to accomplish this. These have been proven quite successful over the years, in thousands of calls. I call these techniques Call Metronome, Telephone Personality, and Script Encoding. This part is actually quite fun, so kick back and enjoy!

Call Metronome

Guess how first impressions are made? C'mon. Guess. Eighty percent of the impression someone gets of you comes from your body language. Seven percent comes from what you say and thirteen percent comes from how you say it.

Twice as important as what you say is how you say it.

Over the telephone, most of your impression is made in the first few seconds. Scary thought. It doesn't give you a lot of time to win someone over, does it? I don't know if you've ever ridden a horse, but if you have, you know that your horse will sense whether you're a novice or an experienced rider (just who is taking whom for a ride, buddy?), just from the way you approach and mount. Your prospects will also have you pegged in seconds flat. In the first few seconds the tone of your voice will send signals that reveal your level of confidence, energy, enthusiasm, sincerity, and professionalism. How you come across in a matter of seconds will determine whether or not your prospect will be receptive to what you have to say.

I discovered a long time ago that, believe it or not, how

you say your first two words (Good morning/afternoon/evening) will determine how the rest of your dialogue will turn out.

How you start is how you finish.

If your first words are rushed, you're going to rush your whole patter. This might surprise you, but the number-one reason why people will turn you down is that you talk too fast. The person you are calling might be in the middle of ten things and won't hear what you're saying. Have you ever had someone stop you at the end of your introduction by asking, "What did you say your name was again?" You were talking too fast. Since every word you speak paints an image in the mind of the person you are calling, let them picture each and every word. After all, you crafted each word for a reason, right?

The slower you talk, the more people listen.

You not only must be heard, but you must also be taken seriously. When you speak slowly you send a message that what you have to say is important. (Have you ever heard royalty speak quickly?) It sends a message of supreme confidence. When you say your name slowly you send a message that you are important.

You need to maintain an even pace throughout your first thirty seconds; not too fast and not too slow. Just an average talking speed. (Would you buy anything from a fast talking salesperson?) You want to remain in control, which means speaking deliberately and confidently. If the person you are speaking with speaks quickly, it's acceptable to pick up your pace once you open up the conversation, but under no circumstances should your opening thirty seconds be rushed. Remember, you have to be heard and taken seriously.

Speaking slowly is only part of the picture. Your energy

level also sends an important message. Energy is contagious and helps convey that you are passionate about what you are saying. An energetic "good morning" also ensures that your energy level will be up for the rest of your conversation. A word of caution here. Coming across with lots of energy and enthusiasm doesn't mean that you have to scream or sound insincere. On the contrary, energy and enthusiasm should be natural. It should sound like a greeting you would give a neighbor on the very first day of spring.

Pacing and energy are just two of four measurements you should gauge when working on your delivery. The other two are the degrees to which you sound passionate and conversational. Passion can come from the way you emphasize a word (see Script Encoding in this section). It is also the result of believing in your offering, and taking the time to focus, before your call, on the value you bring to the table (see the Call Caffeine® section for techniques). Sounding conversational is simple. The call is only a conversation between two people, so you should never sound like you are reading from a script, even if you are. When you focus before the call on who you are calling, especially what the person sounds and looks like, you are more likely to be more conversational. To get you started on the road to a conversational delivery, record your script into your voicemail and then play it back after an hour. Voicemail tells it like it is. If you sound conversational, you are. If not, try again, perhaps speaking your script from memory this time rather than reading it. Never make an actual call until you are certain you sound completely conversational.

Telephone Personality

Since people buy from people, not companies, the personality you portray is essential to your success. Yet your audience has less than thirty seconds — without the aid of body language — to get a sense of what your personality is. Everyone has a distinct telephone personality. You can appear to be any type of person you choose to be; it's all in your control. Now, I'm not suggesting for a moment that you be someone you are not. On the contrary, I want you to be yourself, but be aware that you can create a separate and distinct telephone personality for the duration of your call.

So just what kind of personality do you want to convey? For example, often when I'm calling a president of a large corporation I remind myself that I too am the president of a company. By putting the image of company president in my mind, I begin to focus on the fact that I'm simply calling a peer. That causes me instantly to sound more authoritative. That's the really interesting part of this exercise.

You have the power to change your tone by changing the image in your mind.

For example, many people I coach find that their tone on the call instantly becomes more conversational and relaxed when they visualize themselves speaking with the prospect in the prospect's office, often just imagining that they are sitting across the prospect's desk. To sound more friendly and confident some people simply imagine that the person on the other end of the phone is expecting their call. I myself always imagine that the person I am calling is already a customer, they just don't know it yet. That simple visualization creates an instant rapport since I sound like I've known the person all my life. I'm also more casual because if they are already customers, there is no pressure. I come across genuinely happy to share an opportunity, much like someone smiling before they surprise you with a gift.

Script Encoding

What can give you the ability and confidence to say your dialogue with the perfect delivery every time? Script encoding: the art of placing emphasis on words by using *sonic traffic signs*. You know how regular traffic signs work, telling you when to go, when to stop, and when to yield? Well, sonic traffic signs are little markings carefully placed on selected words, indicating precisely when to pause, where to place emphasis, and how much emphasis to use.

As you know, every word you speak paints an image in your prospect's mind. Picture those powerful images in black and white. What would happen if a few of those images were in color? They'd stand out, wouldn't they? The emphasis you place on any given word turns it from a black and white image into color, giving you the power to make people listen to what you have to say.

ENCODING TABLE
Bold
Bold
<u>Underline</u>
/

The sonic traffic signs are: **<u>bold underline</u>, bold,** <u>underline</u>, and slash /. **<u>Bold underline</u>** is used *sparingly,* usually just on words where you want to place the most emphasis, like "Good morning," where you need the most energy and enthusiasm. **Bold** is applied on words that need less emphasis than bold underline (by about half) but fifty percent more emphasis than you would use on unencoded words (words that have not been specially marked with these sonic traffic signs). A word in bold would typically mean that you would either raise your volume a bit or lower it slightly. (Speaking softly on a word packs a lot of punch.) You could also use a word in bold to stretch it, such as the word "more" becoming "morrrre". <u>Underlined</u> words receive half the emphasis of words that are bolded or, in other words, about twenty-five percent more emphasis than unencoded words. This is the same emphasis as when you normally raise your pitch on a word. As for the slash, that's your stop sign (a half-second pause).

Whenever you pause in a conversation, either face to face or over the telephone (where the pause is magnified as in radio) a half-second of silence at just the right word draws people towards you, makes them listen and focus on that word or thought, or gives them the opportunity to absorb an important point.

The art comes in knowing which words need emphasis. That's a strategic decision. Whatever words you emphasize, choose them carefully because your audience will zero in on any word you emphasize. You don't want to overdo it. *Be selective.* Use the sonic traffic signs sparingly. The following exercise is designed to help you practise listening to how emphasis and pausing affect your message, and to help you know when something sounds off and when it sounds right.

Read the following out loud (record yourself if you wish), emphasizing the **bold** word in each line. (You can add emphasis by speaking louder or softer.)

I'd like to help you organize your day and save you time.
I'd **like** to help you organize your day and save you time.
I'd like to **help** you organize your day and save you time.
I'd like to help **you** organize your day and save you time.
I'd like to help you **organize** your day and save you time.
I'd like to help you organize **your** day and save you time.
I'd like to help you organize your day **and** save you time.
I'd like to help you organize your day and **save** you time.
I'd like to help you organize your day and save you **time.**

Which **bolded** word makes the sentence sound more commanding? Bold up the most effective word in the line below.

I'd like to help you organize your day and save you time.

Where does it make sense to <u>underline</u> words for emphasis? (Remember, it's about half the emphasis of bold.) Try your luck on the line below.

I'd like to help you organize your day and save you time.

Now mix <u>underline</u> and **bold** in the same sentence, where appropriate. (What does it sound like?)

I'd like to help you organize your day and save you time.

Now pause for a moment . . .

Read the following out loud, pausing at the slashes.

I'd / like to help you organize your day and save you time.
I'd like to / help you organize your day and save you time.
I'd like to help you / organize your day and save you time.
I'd like to help you organize your / day and save you time.
I'd like to help you organize your day and / save you time.
I'd like to help you organize your day and save you / time.

Rewrite the above sentence placing the emphasis where it sounds best to you. (I want to make sure you have a good feel for how powerful a single pause carefully placed can be, and how damaging it can be if overused or not placed correctly.)

_____

_____

_____

When you emphasize words you knowingly or unknow-ingly spark certain reactions. Here's an example of how emphasis on a different word can create a different response:

You:	This approach will yield additional <u>savings</u> of ten per cent.
Prospect:	I get savings now.
You:	This approach will yield <u>additional</u> savings of ten per cent.
Prospect:	How much more?

Once you observe that you are creating a particular response, be prepared to control that response with an effective reply. This also sends the message that you are confident.

Placing emphasis on a certain word can also help you sound more passionate. Read the two examples below out loud (note the bold followed by a pause) and observe how much more passionate you sound.

I know that I can help you save more money.

I know / that I can help you save more money.

Got the hang of it? Assuming you have your telephone commercial ready, write it down below.

Opening dialogue (unencoded):

_____

_____

_____

_____

_____

_____

Now record yourself reading the dialogue. Stop the tape when you are done. Do not rewind. Now rewrite your opening dialogue and encode it with sonic traffic signs. Take your time. It takes time to get it right.

_____
_____
_____
_____
_____
_____

Rehearse the above encoded dialogue until you think you have it perfect, then record again. After recording, rewind the tape to the beginning and listen to the difference between your unencoded and encoded versions. Note the differences below:

_____
_____
_____
_____
_____
_____
_____

There is a definite art to script encoding. It can often take hours just to encode a few lines, because you have to try each word separately to get a feel for how it sounds. If a word doesn't need any extra emphasis or a pause, don't use it. Too much encoding will destroy your delivery. Just the right amount, carefully placed and executed, will enhance your delivery beyond your wildest dreams.

Once you have encoded to your satisfaction, rehearse your lines until you sound completely natural and conversational. It's worth repeating: it is imperative that you sound conversational at all times. If a word needs to be emphasized but it does not sound conversational, first check to see if the type of emphasis needs to be changed. If that still does not deliver a natural sounding word or phrase, then skip the encoding where it does not sound natural. No one should ever know that you are reading from a script. In fact, the phone call should sound transparent. You should simply sound as natural as if you were talking to the prospect in person. When it's right, you'll know it.

Shakespeare's got nothing on you, kid . . .

6

Call Caffeine

*T*he longest distance between two points is often the one between you and your telephone. You can have the best intentions in the world, not be afraid of anything, and even be anxious to get started, but the moment you reach for the telephone, what happens? Exactly. Not much. Chances are you don't even make it to the telephone. There are thousand other things you'd rather be doing, and there's never a better time to do them than when you have to pick up the telephone. What's the word I'm looking for here? PROCRASTINATION. It comes from two Latin words, "*pro*" (for) and "*crastinus*" (tomorrow), which pretty much sums up when you'd like to take care of your telephone sales calls! What's your favorite excuse? Don't be shy, you've got a hundred of them. We all do. If you work in an office, see if any of these ring a bell:

24 Famous Excuses for Not Picking Up the Telephone

1. *Open mail.*
2. *Send mail.*
3. *Get a coffee.*
4. *Catch up on voicemail.*
5. *Catch a meeting.*
6. *Set up a meeting.*
7. *Send a memo.*
8. *Get a refill on coffee.*
9. *Return calls.*
10. *Call a friend.*
11. *Call a supplier.*
12. *Clear your desk.*
13. *File incoming bills (but don't pay them).*
14. *Get a muffin for your coffee.*
15. *Read the newspaper.*
16. *Read the business section of the newspaper.*
17. *Read any section of the newspaper.*
18. *Go find that missing section of the newspaper.*
19. *Go to the bathroom (one of the joys of coffee).*
20. *Check e-mail on your way back from the bathroom.*
21. *Write a report.*
22. *Surf the Net.*
23. *Pay those bills (you're clearly desperate by now).*
24. *Start back at 1, pass "Go," and don't collect a contract.*

If you work from home, here's a special list just for you:

12 Famous Excuses for Not Picking Up the Telephone at Home

1. *Go to the refrigerator.*
2. *Feed the cat.*
3. *Turn on the stereo.*
4. *Get the mail and check for your favorite magazine.*
5. *Feed the cat again.*
6. *Head for the refrigerator again in case you missed something the first time around.*
7. *Spy on the neighbor.*
8. *Check for junk mail piling up on the porch.*
9. *Actually read that awful junk mail and pretend it's useful.*
10. *Go back to the refrigerator.*
11. *Make out a grocery list because there's nothing left in the refrigerator.*
12. *Feed the cat.*

(Ever notice how people who work from home have fat cats?)

Seriously now, take another look at that inventory of activities (busy, aren't we?) and tell me which one of them actually makes you money! Seems to me that you'd be better off filling your time doing something that generates sales. That's what you're in business for. And that, I might add, is what telephone sales calls do best — they make sales happen! That's why being motivated to pick up that telephone is so critical. It's safe to say that *motivation is the biggest factor in your success.* Motivation not only affects your ability to pick up the telephone, but it is also a big factor in how effective you are once you're on the telephone.

Recently a sales director at a Fortune 500 company was joking with me, asking, "Why is it that salespeople are always huddled around in doughnut shops complaining about the fact that they can't get leads?" Why indeed.

Picking up the telephone to make sales calls is not a problem for people who are naturally motivated. But for the rest of the population, it's the single greatest obstacle they face in starting the process.

What does it mean to be motivated? It means acknowledging what I call the Motivation FEE (Focus, Energy, Enthusiasm). *Motivation is a state of mind and a state of body.* You want to feel good and enthusiastic about something you are doing, and feeling this way increases your energy level. In fact, there is an interesting relationship between energy and enthusiasm: You need one to get the other. Energy requires enthusiasm, and enthusiasm feeds your energy. Have you ever heard of anyone who was motivated and lethargic?

People are attracted to others who display energy and enthusiasm. It's contagious, both in person and over the telephone. But energy and enthusiasm are especially critical when using the telephone because you have to compensate for the lack of body language, where eighty percent of your initial impression is made.

Motivation is also about being focused, because if you lose your focus, you can lose the call. Specifically, you have to be highly focused on who you are calling, and why you are calling them.

Who Are You Calling?

When was the last time you got a call from a telemarketer who sounded like they were calling a number, not a person? Most telemarketers are not focused on *who* they are calling, namely you as a real live individual. "Who are you calling?" means focusing on the person behind the number. Back in an earlier discussion on the fear of technology I showed that the telephone can make your interaction with people very impersonal. To personalize the call (that is, to get a feel for the person you are calling), what you need to do to is focus on who you are calling by familiarizing yourself with the person you are speaking with: what the person looks, sounds, and acts like. Even focus on your relationship with that person.

Why Are You Calling?

Focusing on why you are calling means focusing on your *call objective.* If you don't focus on asking for an appointment, you'll never get around to it, or stumble if you do. You also want to focus on *the value you bring to the person and company you are calling.* How will your products/services help them achieve their goals and objectives? If you can't get excited about what you're offering, you will never sound convincing, and you will always find it more difficult to pick up the telephone. Lastly, you want to focus on *how the end result will help you realize your goals/dreams.* This is not just because focusing on success ensures your success. It's more fundamental than that. To reach the point where you *want* to pick up the telephone, there has to be something in it for you. There has to be a real, tangible payoff. Focusing on your pot of gold at the end of the rainbow is a definite incentive.

Mustering high levels of energy and enthusiasm while staying focused is particularly challenging when you are making dozens of calls one after the other, sometimes day after day. The solution is to condition yourself to be motivated automatically, at a moment's notice, so that you can maintain a highly motivated state with minimum amount of effort. Will you be able to? You bet. Just reach for some of my Call Caffeine, a series of fourteen highly effective motivational techniques.

Call Caffeine is based on the premise that when you are not motivated it's because you have lost energy, enthusiasm, or focus — or some combination thereof. By discovering where the root cause of your problem lies, you learn how to fix it, assuming you know the proper techniques. That's where Call Caffeine comes in. Each technique is designed to *restore energy, enthusiasm, and focus*, or any combination that you are likely to need.

You can alternate the numerous Call Caffeine techniques as often as required to suit your changing moods. The more you apply these techniques, the less time it takes to be motivated the next time around. Eventually you will reach a point where your motivation turns on automatically. Try all the techniques and use the ones that work best for you.

To help you determine which techniques to apply at any given moment, I have created two kinds of charts for easy reference. The first highlights Call Caffeine techniques in terms of Focus, Energy, and Enthusiasm. But until you get to the point where you can intuitively feel what ails you, the second chart is laid out with more general kinds of problems you may experience and their appropriate Call Caffeine solutions.

Call Caffeine® Motivational Techniques

	Motivation **FEE** *Table*
Focus	**F**
Energy	**E**
Enthusiasm	**E^2**
1. *Believe in What You're Selling*	**F E E^2**
2. *Think Hot Calls*	**E^2**
3. *Double Cream All Sugar*	**F**
4. *Pot of Gold*	**F**
5. *Personal Success Journal*	**F E^2**
6. *Repeat Past Success*	**F E E^2**
7. *Prophecy*	**F**
8. *Dreams*	**F E E^2**
9. *Friends*	**F E E^2**
10. *All Clear*	**F**
11. *Yes!*	**E**
12. *Break Out!*	**E**
13. *Familiar Places*	**F E E^2**
14. *Rewards*	**F E E^2**

1. Believe in What You're Selling

I can't begin to tell you how many hundreds of people I have spoken to who do not believe in what they're selling, and then wonder why they aren't motivated. Motivation begins with a true, passionate belief in what you're selling. When you don't really believe in what you're selling, it comes across on the other end of the telephone in the form of low energy, no enthusiasm, and even less focus. A one-way ticket going nowhere.

On the other hand, when you do believe that what you're selling is going to have a positive effect on people's lives, your energy, enthusiasm, and focus are magnified and, consequently, so are your results.

If you don't believe in what you're selling, pack it in. Find something else to offer that you *can* believe in. When you do, focus on it before you call.

Now, what exactly does it mean to believe in what you're selling? It begins with an understanding of *what* you're selling. You can't believe in something you don't understand. Make sure that you really know everything about your product, service, and company. If you are self-employed, *you* are the product, which means that you have to believe in yourself. Next, know where and how you and your products/services can make a real difference to people and companies. That belief has to translate into real excitement about what you're selling. Excitement turns into energy and enthusiasm. Hey, if you have something that makes people's lives better, why shouldn't you spread the word?

Complete the following exercise and see how you too can become a true believer:

What are you offering companies? (What's the sizzle?)

_____

_____

What is your unique selling proposition?

_____

_____

Where do you feel you can make a real difference to people and companies?

_____

_____

_____

What makes you proud of what you have to offer the world?

_____

_____

_____

On the subject of pride, make sure you feel it, because that's when you'll know that you truly believe in what you're selling. Think of all the people and accomplishments you're proud of. That's how you should feel about what you're offering.

To help you stay focused on all the good things you've done for your customers, take a list of all your satisfied customers and any customer testimonials, and post it on your wall where you can see it. (While you're doing that, remember back in Strategic Scripting, when you wanted to find out what makes you unique, you did an informal poll of your customers? Take their responses and add them to the testimonials.) Reflect on those words you've pinned up, along with other thoughts about your sizzle and unique selling proposition.

Perhaps the most important technique you should apply before every call is to take a minute and reflect on the actual words in your script. Remember, those words not only paint images in the mind of your audience, they also paint images in your mind.

Your words have to turn you on before they can turn others on.

Since your message is tailored to your audience, make sure to research the company and individual you are calling. The more you know about whom you are calling, the more confident and passionate you will be about why you are calling.

2. Think Hot Calls

People will always gravitate towards the mental images they create, and quite often those powerful mental images are created through the use of words. Remember when you were a kid and someone said, "Wipe that smirk off your face?" What did you do? You smirked! You focused on "smirk" and moved in that direction. (What they should have said was, "Let's see you smile." What do you suppose you would have done then?) What's in a word? Plenty. Play this little game with me for a second.

What is a more enticing way to say:

Sparkling white wine?

_____

Chopped liver?

_____

Snails?

_____

Each word draws up a mental image that you respond to emotionally. If you're like most people, champagne sounds more enticing than sparkling wine. Pâté sounds more delicious than chopped liver. And *escargots* does more to whet the appetite than does snails. Indeed, words draw up mental images that can either motivate or de-motivate, depending on your mood.

Hey, now that I've set you up nicely, tell me what comes to mind when you hear the words "Cold Call"? Remember the picture of "telephone sales calls" you drew in chapter two? Have another look. That's the picture you're focusing on every time you hear the words "Cold Call." How can anyone warm up to a cold call? There's nothing positive, enticing, motivating, or exciting in your mental image. With that image in mind, you reach for the telephone and say to yourself, "I'm going to make a cold call." What's wrong with that picture? Say it again. "I'm going to make a cold call." Hear it? A COLD CALL. Brrrrrr. Think about it. You're put off before you even get started. What does the phrase "Cold Call" mean? You freeze up on the telephone and the party on the other end reciprocates with an equally chilling reception! What you need is a different twist of phrase that leaves you with a warmer, more positive mental image.

Before I tell you what that would be, I'd like you to imagine that you're a busy, successful salesperson. (If you're one already, act natural.) One day your boss comes up to you and says, "I've got this lead I'd like you to follow up on. The division doesn't have much money and they're not in a buying mode right now, although they can sure use our services. Call them."

How motivated will you be to call them?

❏ *Very motivated*   ❏ *A little motivated*
❏ *Wouldn't give it any thought*

Now imagine that you're still a busy, successful salesperson. One day your boss comes up to you and says, "I've got this *hot lead* I'd like you to follow up on. The division has buckets of money and they're just reviewing their budgets this month. They sure can use our services. Call them."

How motivated will you be to call them?

❏ *Very motivated*   ❏ *A little motivated*
❏ *Wouldn't give it any thought*

Why?

_____

_____

_____

_____

_____

One lead was cold, while the other was hot. May I suggest that from now on you banish the words "Cold Call" from your vocabulary and substitute them with the phrase "Hot Call." "Hot Call" implies a positive end result — in the same way as a *hot lead* or a *hot* opportunity gets you motivated.

Draw the mental picture that comes to mind when you think of Hot Calls.

┌───┐
│   │
│   │
│   │
│   │
│   │
│   │
│   │
│   │
│   │
│   │
└───┘

What you have drawn is a positive image that creates positive emotions. By using the phrase "Hot Calls" from now on, you will automatically condition yourself to bring back these same motivating feelings — and pick up the telephone a lot faster as a result.

3. Double Cream All Sugar

This simple technique is one of my favorites. As the name suggests, we're talking, quite literally, about a cup of coffee. Two, to be precise. You see, the telephone doesn't allow you to schmooze over a coffee before you speak with the prospect, as you would when you meet someone in person. All the more reason why you have to turn your impersonal call into a personal call (and by doing so, overcome the fear of technology). The Double Cream All Sugar technique gives you the ability to familiarize yourself with the person you're calling. It brings you closer together so that you're not calling a stranger, you're calling someone you think you know because you have a favorable mental picture of the individual. Not only do you feel more connected with the person, but you are also highly focused on the fact that you are calling a real person, not just a telephone number.

It's this simple: Before you call someone, pour two cups of coffee, one for you and one for your prospect, and set the one for the other person in front of you. At that point, simply imagine that you're joining your prospect in their office for a cup of small talk. Don't just gulp down the coffee. There is a specific process for creating that positive mental image. Hey, what can I tell you? Schmoozing is an art.

Here's the process in action:

1. Get two cups of coffee. One's for you, the other is for the person you are about to call.
2. Now place yourself mentally in the prospect's office. Form an impression of:
   - What your prospect looks like
     (If possible, obtain a picture of your prospect from the Web, a newspaper, business publications, or an annual report.)
   - What your prospect sounds like
     (Use the Voicefinder technique the night before.)

- What your prospect's office looks like
  (I find it helpful to check out the prospect's Web site before the call, not only to research the company, but also to see what its logo and headquarters look like. Being able to visualize your prospect's work environment is one more step in personalizing the call, and does wonders for your ability to focus on the person you are calling.)
- The kind of a morning your prospect is having
- How your call will make your prospect's day better.

Then place yourself in the picture sitting down in front of the prospect.

Make the call *now*.

Let's do a trial run. Got the coffee? Double cream and lots of sugar. No, it's OK. I like it good and strong. Oh, and I forgot to mention, you're calling *me*.

Describe what I look like.

_____

_____

Describe what I sound like.

_____

_____

Draw what my office looks like.

Describe what kind of a morning I'm having.

_____

_____

_____

Describe how your call will make my day better.

_____

_____

_____

In the picture you drew moments ago, mentally place yourself in the picture sitting down in front of me. Call me now! Did you feel that you knew me any better? By that I mean did you feel that you were calling a number, or that you were calling a real live person — me?

❏ *A number*   ❏ *A person*
❏ *A person you now know a little better*

Did you feel colder or warmer towards making the call?

❏ *Colder*   ❏ *Warmer*

Practise this exercise a few times before you make some real calls, just to get a sense of how it makes you feel. And by the way, you make a great cup of coffee. If you serve this up again, you can call me anytime.

4. Pot of Gold

Motivation has nothing to do with why people *have* to do anything, but rather, motivation is about why anyone would *want* to do something. "Have to" is not motivating. "Want to" is. One reason why you would want to do something is because there is something in it for you. That might turn out to be a reward of some kind, or a positive end result, or the fulfillment of your goals and dreams. So to help you get into the "want to" frame of mind — as in you want to make Hot Calls — it is particularly motivating to focus on a mental picture of the positive results of your calls. (If you want to get to where you're going, you have to focus on where you're going and see a positive image ahead.) What exactly lies ahead for you when you make Hot Calls? What's the end result? Think of the big picture here. There has to be a positive, achievable goal, something that will inspire you to great things. For example, the following equation might ring true for you. Hot Calls lead to . . .

Hot Calls ➠ *appointments* ➠ *sales* ➠ *profit* ➠ *success* ➠ *the ability to buy what you want, go where you want to go, and become financially independent* ➠ *lifestyle* ➠ *happiness*

What's the pot of gold at the end of the rainbow? *True happiness.* I'd make Hot Calls for a goal like that, wouldn't you? Hot Calls book appointments, which lead to sales, which make you money, which you can reinvest in yourself and your business, which brings in more money leading to greater success providing you with a great lifestyle, which ultimately makes you a happy camper.

What you are doing is giving your mind a more positive picture to focus on. Instead of associating those calls with endless hours of drudgery and uncertainty, you associate Hot Calls with *the certainty of success and happiness.* The new perception leaves you motivated because you see a direct relationship between making Hot Calls and achieving what you want.

Listen, don't let me second-guess what you want. You tell me. What do *you* want? Complete the following equation to demonstrate what Hot Calls lead to:

Hot Calls ➠ ➠ ➠
➠ ➠ ➠

Now draw the pot of gold at the end of your rainbow.

Describe what's in the pot of gold for you.

_____

_____

_____

You have just created for yourself a positive mental picture. Now here's what I'd like you to do with that inspiring vision. (I never make a call without applying this technique first.)

- Before you call people (you never call numbers) on your Hit List, visualize *the whole campaign* taking place. Picture yourself making all the calls, and visualize the positive end result. (Hot Calls lead to appointments, which lead to . . .)
- The next step is to visualize each call *separately* before making the calls. As you picture yourself making each call, visualize the call taking place with you delivering your opening line and then the prospect asking a question or telling you that he's happy with his current supplier; then visualize that you are delivering your passionate (prepared) response and then the person is agreeing to see you; then the next thing you know you're in their office and weeks later they become a satisfied customer.

Then picture another positive end result, with a dream of yours coming true as a result of making that call. In other words, focus on the pot of gold at the end of your rainbow. By visualizing in this manner you are in a state of total focus. Your mind is prepared for anything, and goes on autopilot when a question or objection arises because it has already seen that movie. Your own greed glands light up because your dream is in full view.

Try it now for a moment. Imagine making all the calls on your Hit List, from preparation through to completion. Describe what you see.

_____

_____

_____

_____

Imagine a single call taking place, from preparation through to completion — from the rainbow to the pot of gold. Detail what you see.

_____

_____

_____

_____

5. Personal Success Journal

People are motivated to succeed when they focus on success, and when they learn how small successes lead to larger successes. (In chapter two you also read about how focusing on success helps eliminate the fear of rejection.) Unfortunately, most people tend to forget all the great accomplishments they've made. Allow me to offer this unique remedy: Record your success and keep it close at hand. You might call your record a daily Personal Success Journal. Here's an example of what I mean.

Do yourself a big favor and take a few moments after each successful call to complete your Personal Success Journal. It is a living record of your successes. Imagine how good you will feel when you review it at the end of each day. The sense of accomplishment. The feeling that you are moving forward. How can you not be motivated by the thought that you can succeed and will succeed! When you end every day on an up note like that, you will always be more motivated to continue making your calls tomorrow.

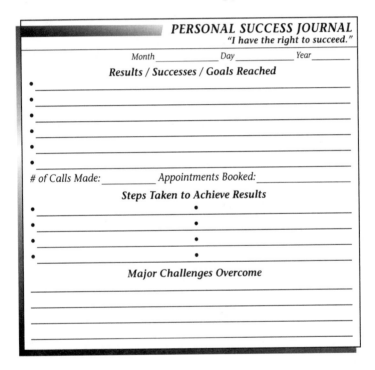

PERSONAL SUCCESS JOURNAL
"I have the right to succeed."

Month_____ Day _____ Year_____

Results / Successes / Goals Reached

• _____
• _____
• _____
• _____
• _____
• _____

# of Calls Made:_____ Appointments Booked:_____

Steps Taken to Achieve Results

• _____ • _____
• _____ • _____
• _____ • _____
• _____ • _____

Major Challenges Overcome

_____
_____
_____
_____

Your Personal Success Journal will also be an inspiration to you the next time you have a difficult problem to overcome. Simply knowing that you overcame a challenge before sets a positive mental image that says you will overcome it again.

Just for the record, list what you have accomplished today.

_____

_____

_____

_____

Describe how you feel about those accomplishments.

_____

_____

_____

_____

6. Repeat Past Success

While we're on the subject of your success, let's build on it. *If you were successful before, you can be successful again, by repeating the actions you took to ensure your success.*

Suppose this were a hot August day, and you were taking one of your leisurely walks through a very large park. You've been walking for hours. Gettin' awful thirsty, I bet. Time to cut out for a cold drink. Right about now, actually. Lucky for you there's a shortcut out of the park, but that means climbing over a fence. A six-foot fence. Wow. How tall did you say you were? If you have never climbed a fence in your life, you probably wouldn't attempt it. Why not? Mostly because you have no reason to believe you can jump it. On the other hand, if you have jumped a fence once before — even as far back as your public-school days when a six-foot fence looked like a hundred-foot fence — you would feel pretty confident about jumping the fence because you had succeeded in doing so once before. In other words, *past success gave you the confidence to assume future success.*

Past success also gave you a point of reference. Standing there reminiscing in front of that six-foot fence, you would instinctively go back into your memory and visualize how you jumped the fence in the past. You would try to recall your physical and mental state. Let's take a walk down memory lane.

Watch out for the fence . . .

Recall the experience when you were a child climbing a fence for the first time. How did you feel when first encountering this challenge?

_____

_____

Which hand did you use first to grab hold of the fence?

❏ *Left*   ❏ *Right*   ❏ *Both*

Did you jump off from your left foot or your right foot?

❏ *Left*   ❏ *Right*

Did you stand up close before jumping, or take a running start?

❏ *Close*   ❏ *Running*

If you took a running start, how far away from the fence were you?

_____

Did you push yourself up over the top using your arms, or did you have enough momentum from jumping to clear the top?

❏ *Arm strength*   ❏ *Momentum*

Did you land on both feet at the same time?

❏ *Yes*   ❏ *No*

How did you feel after you completed your jump and cleared the fence?

_____
_____
_____

If you have jumped a fence before, you know you can do it again because you have the confidence and the *strategy to succeed.* (Just repeat the very actions you detailed and you should clear the fence without a problem.) Now let's get back to those Hot Calls. The next time you find yourself lacking some focus, energy, and enthusiasm, think about past calls that were successful.

What made them successful?

_____
_____
_____
_____

What time of day did you make the calls?_____

What steps did you take to ensure success (scripting, call planning, motivation, etc.)?

_____
_____
_____
_____

What were you thinking about or concentrating on before and during those calls?

_____
_____
_____
_____

Draw how you felt as you were making those successful calls.

Describe how you felt *after* you made those successful calls.

_____

_____

_____

_____

Review your Personal Success Journal if you need more inspiration or ideas from your past successes. The fact that you know that you were successful before will give you the confidence to make the calls and be successful again. By reliving both *the mental and physical states* you were in when you made successful calls, you will have the strategies for succeeding once again. (And by focusing on success, you will push yet another stake into the heart of that fear of rejection.)

7. Prophecy

When I was a young pup of eight, my mother tried to quit smoking. She succeeded by using an interesting technique. Every time she lit up a cigarette, Mother said out loud to herself, "This cigarette is killing me." Over a period of months she gradually lost interest in smoking and, one day, stopped altogether. That episode obviously stuck in my mind all these years, and later in life I used Mother's technique to help me make successful Hot Calls.

What Mother had done was to create such a negative mental image of smoking (by verbalizing it) that she eventually moved in the direction of that picture. Where have we heard that concept before? What I have done since then is to make sure that every time I pick up the telephone to make sales calls, I verbally express either my call objective or my pot of gold. For example, I will say things like, "This call is going to result in an appointment" or "This call is going to get me a vacation." This has helped me succeed in several ways. First, it keeps me focused on my call objective, so that I never forget to ask for the appointment. Secondly, it keeps me motivated by focusing on a positive end result. In other words, I always make sure that I paint a *positive mental picture* in my head (remember that we all move in the direction of our mental images), whether it is the thought of an appointment, or the thought of what that appointment will lead to.

In the long run, *verbalizing* a goal transforms that objective and mental image into a self-fulfilling prophecy. Over the years of using this technique, many of my holidays have been paid for by the sales that resulted from those calls. My advice to you is that whenever you need help focusing on why you are calling (the call objective and the realization of your dreams), simply go to the telephone, pick it up, and verbalize your call objective or a dream, such as, "This call is going to result in an appointment," or "This call is going to get me that home in Bermuda."

For best results, use the Prophecy Call Caffeine technique just before you say "Good morning." It gets you good and focused for your Call Metronome.

8. Dreams

It's Saturday afternoon. The kids are out playing. Sounds like the perfect time to put your feet up and have a cool drink. Ahhhh. Hey, where's your favorite magazine? That's better. Isn't it inspiring to look at all those fantastic pictures? You're not the only person to live your dreams through all those expensive photographs. Looking at pictures of your dreams makes you feel good. Inspired. Puts you in a positive frame of mind. Increases your energy. Now why on earth would you want to go and do all that?

Dreams are powerful motivators. The problem is they tend to feel distant and abstract. They are always "out there" somewhere and referred to in the future tense. Think how much more motivating your dreams would be if they were in the present tense. Dreams are powerful motivators when they are seen as achievable and close at hand. Try this little experiment:

What would you do if you won a million dollars in a lottery?

_____

_____

_____

Describe in the greatest of detail what you would buy.

_____

_____

_____

_____

_____

Before you go any further, go out and buy a lottery ticket. I'll wait . . .

That was fast. How much is the draw for? That's a lot of money! Put your lottery ticket on the desk or table in front of you right now, then do the following:

Describe in the greatest of detail what you would buy if you won.

_____

_____

_____

_____

_____

After you've completed the answer, compare what you wrote with your response to the same question earlier on. Which one has more detail? Having the lottery ticket in your hand made your dream turn from abstract to concrete. You could touch it. See it. Hold it. Your dream stopped being a dream and started becoming something that was possible. Then it got really exciting, didn't it?

To make your dreams motivate you at this very moment, you need to have a visual representation of that dream right in front of you. Take a second and visualize a dream you hold near and dear to your heart. Inspired? How's your energy level? Now go get an actual picture that represents your dream and take a good look at it. See how much more emotional you get looking at your dream? How's your energy level now? The more real your dreams seem, the more achievable they become. The more achievable, the more motivating.

One consultant I was coaching told me that his dream was to buy a Jaguar. I asked the fellow to get a poster of the car from the dealer or a magazine and cut it into four even parts. Each time his commissions moved him twenty-five percent closer to buying the car, he was to post a quarter of the picture up on the wall in his office. You can imagine how he felt when the first section went up, then half was displayed, then three-quarters, and then finally the whole poster. Yes, he got the Jaguar in the end, or should I say, he motivated himself to earn it.

The next time you feel the need to focus on why you are calling (achieve your dreams/goals), and to boost your energy and enthusiasm, keep a series of motivational pictures in your office, or wherever you'll be calling from. Change the picture daily or weekly to keep the excitement going.

To enhance the effectiveness of this Call Caffeine technique, add visualization. In other words, don't just look at a picture of something that inspires you, *live* it by invoking all your senses. Let's practise this one together.

Personally, I like riding horses in the Rockies, and I tend to keep inspiring photographs of horses and mountains around me when I make my Hot Calls. I've got one in front of me now. I can clearly see those amazing horses and the breathtaking mountains. But let's go further, and tune into the *sounds* those pictures make, like the sound of feet fitting into leather stirrups . . .

Snap

the sound of horses running in a field . . .

frrrump, frrrump, frrrump

the sound of the wind rushing through the mountains . . .

shhhhhhhhhhhhooooooo

I can *smell* the air redolent of pine and the fresh scent a mountain rain shower leaves behind. I can just *taste* the ice-cold mountain water rushing from the falls. I can *feel* my legs wrapping around the body of the horse as I settle down in the saddle for the first time. At this point I'm not just thinking about my dream, I'm there! In this heightened state of motivation, I make my Hot Calls. Having these breathtaking pictures nearby means my dreams are never far away. They are just at the end of my desk.

Time to bring *your* dreams within reach. Get a picture of your dream, and place it in front of you. If you don't have a picture handy, do the visualization solo.

Describe in great detail what your favorite dream is.

_____

_____

_____

Close your eyes and imagine what your dream:

- Looks like
- Sounds like
- Feels like
- Tastes like
- Smells like

Now describe in words what your dream . . .

Looks like:

_____

Sounds like:

_____

Feels like:

_____

Tastes like:

_____

Smells like:

_____

Take a good look at that picture of your dream and make it real. That's worth a telephone call, isn't it?

9. Friends

One day last year I received a panic call from a call center manager in a service bureau where I'd been doing some training in outbound sales. "Steve, you have to help me. Remember Susan, my best rep? She's always a bundle of energy and, you know, really enthusiastic — well, she's having an off-day. It's not like her. Susan's still enthusiastic, but somehow she's not connecting with the customers. She's not handling any of the calls right. I'm concerned. Can you speak with Susan and find out why she's not motivated?" I wiped the sweat from his brow off my receiver, and patched through to Susan who, as the manager said correctly, was always a bundle of energy.

Even before I spoke with her, I knew that since Susan still had her energy and enthusiasm, her uncharacteristically poor performance must be a focus issue. So I asked Susan a few questions to find out whether she had lost focus on who she was calling or why she was calling. As it turned out, it was both. Susan had begun to call numbers. She had lost her focus on the people she was calling. On top of that, she hadn't given any thought to the real value of what she was delivering. Knowing that, I asked Susan what she would say if she were calling a friend. Well, surprise, surprise! After telling me how she would call up a friend, her approach and tone changed for the better; right in the middle of her description, she laughed out loud and said, "Steven, that's really neat. I'd never thought of my prospects as friends!" After our conversation, Susan went on making her usual successful calls for the rest of the day.

(Susan's ability to focus on her prospects as friends transformed an otherwise impersonal call into a personal call, which, as it turned out, gave her motivation and performance a much needed boost.)

To help focus on who you are calling and why, treat the person you are calling not as a stranger, but as a friend. (To help you visualize the person you are calling, add your Double Cream All Sugar and Voicefinder techniques.) This turns an impersonal call into a personal call and, on a deeper level, it changes your performance by changing your beliefs. When you believe that you are calling a friend, your expectation is that your friend can't wait to hear from you, so your attitude becomes more positive, and you get excited about speaking with that person. Your energy and enthusiasm go way up, which makes the person you are calling all the more receptive to what you have to say.

Now we all know that you aren't really calling friends. But keep in mind that the mental images you create affect your performance. Allow me to demonstrate — just between friends.

One day you find yourself in a children's bookstore that specializes in pop-up books. You are so amazed at the quality, selection, and price that you have to share it with all your friends who have children. What will you tell your friends?

_____

_____

_____

_____

I bet you were fairly descriptive. I would also wager that you would be very enthusiastic in your manner. The reason for this is not just that you know the person — it's a friend of yours — but that you were not selling the person anything. You were *sharing*. The shift in focus from selling to sharing brings out your passion. Sharing sends a signal that you believe so strongly that what you are offering is of such great value to the other person, that you simply have to tell them. In your mind, you're not selling them anything, you're actually doing them a favor by mentioning it. Whenever you do someone a favor, you feel good, don't you? And when you feel good, you want to do it again.

What would happen if your best friend had never heard about your product or service? Imagine calling your friend to share it right now. What would you tell your friend? Write it down word for word:

_____

_____

_____

_____

Now say it out loud as if your friend was standing in front of you at this very moment. Take the enthusiasm you just demonstrated and repeat that identical performance on your next call.

10. All Clear

If you are not already sitting at your desk (the one with the telephone on it), I'd like you to walk over there and plunk yourself down, without losing your spot on this page. Are you there yet? Good. Let's see how creative you are.

In the following box draw and number all the items on your desk. (You can leave out your stapler, paper clips, and three-hole punch.)

If every item on your desk could talk, each would be screaming for your attention. Using the lines below, write what each item is saying to you at this very moment.

"_____"

"_____"

"_____"

"_____"

"   "
"   "
"   "
"   "
"   "

What is all that stuff on there anyway? What's it doing there? A cluttered desk is a cluttered mind. The only thing you should be concentrating on when you're making Hot Calls is, well, making Hot Calls, and nothing else. What you really have on your desk are a lot of distractions. That stuff is just *screaming* at you for attention. Listen to it: "Pay this." "Call me back." "Finish this report." "Read me." "Read me first." "Don't listen to them, read me!" What a chorus! It's impossible to concentrate on booking those appointments when you're staring at distractions. Everything on your desk is a reason *not to call.* You might as well just put a big sign over your desk that reads *Procrastination Zone!*

Clear your desk. If you're one of those people who can't work on a clean desk (I believe you refer to it as an *organized* mess), put the mess back after your calls. It's worth it. People tell me that they are simply stunned at how their results improve dramatically when their desks are clear. It doesn't surprise me though: Focus is everything!

When you're making Hot Calls, put everything else on hold. There are only five things you should have on your desk:

1. An inspiring picture.
2. An open appointment book (and Hot-Call Travel Planner, if applicable). This tells your mind that you're already going to get those appointments. Seeing is believing. Looking at the daytimer makes the appointment real to you, which makes it believable. If you believe you will book an appointment, you will.

3. A single sheet of paper. On it is printed the name of your prospect, and nothing else. Notice you don't have your Hit List there. All those people staring at you will only shout "Call me first." The natural thing to do is panic. "I have to call all these people? Before 9:30? Ahhhhhhhhhhhh!" Skip the coronary. Just gaze upon the name of the one person you are about to call and impress at this very moment. This will also help you overcome any fear of technology, by personalizing the call.

4. Two coffee mugs. Had your morning coffee yet? Have one cup for you and the other for your prospect. Double Cream All Sugar.

5. Your telephone. (Your ticket to personal success.)

There's no time like the present. Clear you desk right now and see what a difference it makes. Shhhhhhhh! Listen . . . hear that? Neither do I. The chorus has gone home. No distractions. Nothing standing in the way of your achieving your dreams. Now repeat after me, "This call will result in an appointment . . ."

Note: There are two other forms of distractions that require an "All Clear" sign: People trying to reach you on the telephone while you are making a Hot Call, and individuals knocking on your door. The solutions: Don't answer incoming calls while you are already in the middle of a Hot Call. (If you have a feature on the telephone that lets you know someone else is calling while you are on the line — often by way of a subtle beep in your ear — just ignore it.) As for discouraging people who want to talk to you in your office, simply put up a sign on the outside of your door that reads "I'm on the phone" so that your colleagues will leave you undisturbed.

Please allow me to indulge in my favorite All Clear story.

A salesperson named Elizabeth who I was coaching last month told me that thanks to Hot Calls she now stands when speaking on the phone (with a headset) so she can use her hands freely when speaking. She also keeps her desk clear. Elizabeth was astonished at how much more effective she was. She went on to say, "The only problem, Steven, is that even though my desk is clear my floor is a disaster," at which point I said, "Then don't look down!"

11. Yes!

Freeze! If you're sitting down, don't move a muscle. I'm serious. Are you slouching? Aha! How's your energy? Could be better? Hey, don't move yet, you'll ruin this demonstration . . .

Motivation is about energy, and lots of it. Whenever possible, make your calls while standing up. Why? *No one has ever fallen asleep standing up.* When you feel you must sit, don't slouch. Sit up straight and breath from your diaphragm. Good posture gives you energy. Bad posture zaps it. Whenever you catch yourself slouching, throw your arms up in the air, snap your fingers, and say in a loud voice with a burst of energy — Yes! And as you do, sit up good and straight. (Push that back into your chair. Pull that tummy in. Plant those feet squarely on the ground.)

Try it now, on the count of three. (You're still frozen, I take it . . .)

One . . . two . . .

. . . don't move yet . . .

three! *Yes!*

How's your energy now? Feel the surge? Feel more alert? That's the state of a motivated person. Let's keep you that way. And hey, if you forget to catch yourself slouching, get into the habit of checking your clock every half hour or hour, and as you do . . . Yes!

In the meantime, try to make all your calls standing up. Then you're really ready to go places.

12. Break Out!

A break is an oasis along the journey of making successful Hot Calls. More than just a pause, a break is a chance to refuel, re-energize. What I'd like to do is introduce you to a new break concept. I'm not talking about those moments when you need to satisfy physiological needs. I want you to break out of the ordinary. Break to stimulate!

In other words, start taking working breaks. These are breaks with a specific purpose, designed to help you reach your goals. The idea is to plan and schedule specific activities that will boost your supply of energy, enthusiasm, and focus.

Break Intervals:
We live in a society where everything is Go, Go, Go and no one stops to respect their body clock. Like it or not, your body needs a rest at certain times of the day, depending on the type of person you are. Ask yourself, "Am I a morning person or a night person?" Morning people find that they have the most energy early in the day, when they are most alert. While they are more productive in the morning, these people tend to slow down in the afternoon. Morning people hate working at night.

Night people, on the other hand, love working at night, and tend to drive their spouses and friends who are morning people crazy by wanting to stay up late to party. In the morning they need intravenous coffee to generate a pulse. It takes a lot of effort to go to work — unless they have the afternoon or night shift — and they need a lot of time in the morning to get their night-vision eyes focused on the rest of the day.

Once, doing an environmental audit for a call center at a large telephone company, I came across a customer service representative who had just come off the telephone. I approached the young woman and said, "You're a morning person, aren't you?" "How did you know?" she said, surprised. "It takes one to know one," I replied with a smile. I proceeded to tell her that she was probably getting her big break in the morning when, in fact, she would prefer to have it around 2:00 in the afternoon. I was right again. Being a morning person myself, I knew that this person didn't need a break in the morning, but rather in the afternoon, and the result was frustration and a lack of energy. Since every call is important, I advised the center to make the breaks more flexible.

If you're a morning person, plan on taking more breaks in the afternoon.

If you're a night person, you'll need more breaks in the morning. Plan on it.

Break Duration:
Give yourself extended breaks after lengthy call campaigns. The more energy you spend, the more time you'll need to recoup.

Break Activities:
(If you are taking your break in your office, hold all calls.)

1. Read a business journal or quotes from successful people, listen to motivational tapes (for inspiration).
2. Listen to mellow/classical music (for meditation).
3. Take a power nap or slow, deep breaths (for relaxation).
4. Go for a ten-minute walk (for circulation).
5. Call up a friend (for conversation).

Plan some personal break activities of your own that you can do between your Hot Calls, to achieve the following objectives:

Inspiration:

_____

_____

Meditation:

_____

_____

Relaxation:

_____

_____

Circulation:

_____

_____

Conversation:

_____

_____

(A brief word about "Conversation." Spend your precious time talking to positive people who really believe in you and your ability to achieve great things. Do not, under any circumstances, talk to anyone between calls who has a negative attitude, a pessimistic outlook on life. Winners surround themselves with winners. Positive beliefs ignite energy and enthusiasm. For maximum motivational impact, set up a support group of your peers who are also making Hot Calls. Conversation can be inspiration, too!)

Now pump your breaks!

13. Familiar Places

I don't know anyone who can concentrate and get excited about doing something when they are not comfortable in their environment. On the other hand, why do you suppose that creative people go to great lengths to set up their surroundings in ways that inspire them to great accomplishments? If you are making your calls from home, find a place where you are most comfortable making calls, and then use that place exclusively for that purpose. (If you are making your calls from the office, get into the habit of facing the same direction every time you call, either focusing on a particular picture on your desk or gazing out the window.)

There's more than just the matter of comfort here. By conditioning yourself to make calls from the same place, you automatically condition your mind to get into a "Let's make a Hot Call" frame of mind every time you enter that space.

Describe that part of your home or office which is the most comfortable for making Hot Calls.

_____

_____

What is it about the room that makes it conducive to making Hot Calls?

_____

_____

_____

14. Rewards

OK, you're stuck in the middle of a desert island, located directly under the largest hole in the ozone layer. You have to get outta there as fast as possible before you burn. The problem is, your only ticket out of there is a mule, who for reasons of his own kind of likes the heat and the sand and is in no particular mood to oblige you. What's your strategy? Anytime you want to get your ass in gear, pull out a big carrot.

The big carrot in your case is a reward. Things that get

rewarded get done. Yet how many people reward themselves? A reward is not only something you deserve, it is one of the most important motivators in your arsenal. (You may recall that we first touched on rewards back when we were discussing the fear of rejection, and I asked you to reward yourself every time you learned something new from your mistakes.)

When was the last time you treated yourself to something special for accomplishing a goal? Aha. Thought so. That's too bad, because a reward is most effective motivator known to humanity. When you were a child, didn't your parents give you a candy for being good? OK, maybe that was bribery, but it was still a reward for good behavior, and it encouraged good behavior.

Rewarding yourself motivates you to attempt the kinds of activities that need to get done in order to be successful. Rewards also make your successes all the more enjoyable.

Question: When to reward?

Answer: Reward for those activities that lead to success (so that you'll be encouraged to do them) and reward for success itself (getting appointments and sales), so that you'll stay motivated to reach your goals. The sweeter success tastes, the more of it you'll want.

Let me tell you how I reward myself. I love my espresso coffee every morning. I don't need an excuse to pour myself a cup — or do I? After I make my Hit List for the day, I reward myself with an espresso. As soon as I book an appointment, I go for a really good (a.k.a. expensive) lunch. When I get a contract, I treat myself to a very expensive dinner. And guess what I do after 365 days of work? You got it. I've earned a holiday, and I reward myself with a trip to the Rockies for some horseback riding. It's not a holiday. It's a reward for putting in a year of effort. Here's the distinction: A holiday I can cancel anytime. A reward, never. I've never missed a trip to the Rockies.

In the process, what I'm doing is *conditioning* myself to undertake the activities that need to get done, and to achieve the results. I condition myself to be motivated by thinking about the rewards. Most of the time I want to get the appointment just so that I can reward myself with the expensive lunch.

Now think about the following questions:

When do *you* reward yourself at work?

_____

How often do you reward yourself?

_____

How do you reward yourself?

_____
_____
_____

How do you feel when you reward yourself?

_____
_____

Are you rewarding the activities that lead to success? Do you reward yourself with things that you really like, as opposed to things you need? If rewarding yourself makes you feel good, you should be doing it more often. If you're not rewarding yourself often enough, you're probably not getting the results you want often enough.

Where do you go from here? Why not create a personal incentive plan of your own. Begin by answering the following questions:

Name three things you wish you had more time for.

1. _____
2. _____
3. _____

Name some things you would like to do that you have never done before.

_____

_____

_____

Take your answers and create some exciting reward possibilities.

_____

_____

_____

_____

Now that you know what kind of rewards you would really like, create a reward schedule with escalating value. (The closer you get to achieving your goal, the bigger the reward.) Plan to give yourself smaller-priced rewards for the activities that lead to success (making a Hit List, making calls) and reward yourself with higher-priced items for achieving your goals (booking the appointments, making sales, getting contracts, completing a year in business).

A reward can be something you want to do, somewhere you want to go, something you want to buy, or just time off. One financial consultant told me that the best part of this whole system was that it taught her how to shop guilt-free!

What kinds of suggestions can you come up with for your own Incentive Plan? Remember:

1. Of all the activities that need to be rewarded, the most important is learning from your mistakes. (Remember the story of the fellow who gave his wife a rose every day?)
2. When rewarding yourself for booking your first appointment, hold off getting the reward until later in the day. That's because once you're on a roll you need to leverage the confidence and energy to get other appointments and rewards, like three in a row!

PERSONAL INCENTIVE PLAN	
Goal	**Reward**
❑ *Preparing a Hit List*	
❑ *Calling the first prospect*	
❑ *Learning from mistakes*	
❑ *Booking 1st appointment*	
❑ *Three appointments in a row*	
❑ *Five appointments in a row*	
❑ *First ten appointments booked*	
❑ *First appointment attended*	
❑ *First sale*	
❑ *Largest sale*	
❑ *First ten sales*	
❑ *Year end!*	

Now stick to it. Once you earn a reward, follow through. Don't let yourself be drawn into the "I'm too busy" routine. Rewards are not a luxury. They are not even negotiable. Rewards are serious business. Every top producer I have helped build has told me that over the long term the rewards became the most important part of their success. That's because they kept raising the bar in terms of what they rewarded. This not only made it more challenging, but also got them to strive for loftier goals. Many people have incorporated this reward system into their personal lives, and you can imagine the impact that has had on relationships.

One of the most touching reward stories I have ever heard was from a broker named Philip from the West Coast. Philip had just started in the business one spring when he got on board my training program. For the first three months, every new broker in his firm was expected to bring in around $150,000 in assets per month. But our man Philip had bigger goals for himself. He was so inspired by this system that he set himself a goal of one million dollars in assets per month for the first three months. To make sure he got there, Philip told me up front that his reward for reaching his goal was going to be a trip back to England to visit his mother with his children, who had never seen their grandmother.

That August I heard from Philip. He was calling from the airport. He had brought in a million a month in assets for the first three months, and was on his way with his children to reunite with his mother in England.

Call Caffeine Diagnostics

Keep this motivational tool posted where it's easily accessible. *Whenever* you feel that you have lost energy, enthusiasm, and/or focus, stop what you're doing, identify the problem, and then immediately apply the appropriate Call Caffeine techniques. Problem solved. Resume making successful calls.

CALL CAFFEINE DIAGNOSTICS

Problem	Call Caffeine Techniques
I hate calling a stranger.*	*Double Cream All Sugar (combined with Voicefinder), Friends, All Clear*
I hate it when people turn me down.*	*Personal Success Journal, Repeat Past Success, Rewards*
I've lost focus on who I'm calling.	*Double Cream All Sugar, Friends, All Clear*
I don't know why I'm calling.	*Believe in What You're Selling, Pot of Gold, Prophecy, Dreams, All Clear, Rewards*
I'm running out of steam.	*Yes!, Break Out!*
My confidence sure could use a boost.	*Personal Success Journal, Repeat Past Success*
It feels like the person I'm calling is just a number.	*Double Cream All Sugar, Friends, All Clear*
It's hard to get excited about making calls.	*Think Hot Calls, Believe in What You're Selling, Pot of Gold, Dreams, Friends, All Clear, Yes!, Familiar Places, Rewards*
I wish I could motivate myself faster between calls.	*Pot of Gold, Yes!, Familiar Places*
With a lot of calls to make today, I need to stay motivated for long periods of time.	*Pot of Gold, Dreams, All Clear, Yes!, Break Out!, Familiar Places, Rewards*

* The Call Caffeine techniques enhance but do not replace all the other techniques you learned in the section on overcoming fear.

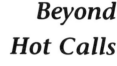

Beyond Hot Calls

*N*ow that you have learned how to make successful Hot Calls, it's time to turn what you've learned into action. Make calls every week, and every day, if you can. The more appointments you book, the more successful you'll be. Start now, whether business is busy or slow.

If things are slow for you right now, making Hot Calls is the one activity that will turn things around for you. At some point, things will start to get busy. Now, you're thinking that with a busy schedule you'll have an excuse for not making any more calls, right?

I think not.

If you're busy, the Hot Calls approach works even better. Most people don't make calls when they're busy. You know what? They're missing out. The best time to call is when you don't have time to make calls. I can't explain why this happens, but whenever you are too busy to see people, that's exactly when they want to see you. The other advantage to calling when you have a lot on your plate is that when you are speaking to prospects over the telephone for the first time, or meeting them in person, you will have a lot of successful things going on that you can tell them about. Prospects want to hire successful people.

Your success will also make your script delivery more effective. When you're busy with lots of work, your energy is up and your enthusiasm is high. You couldn't be better positioned.

But making the Hot Calls is simply the first step in building the customer relationship. After you book your appointments, you will have an opportunity to meet with your prospects, at which point they will either do some business with you on the spot if the timing is right or, if not, they'll leave the door open for you to keep in touch.

Keep in touch.

Ever heard the old adage, "Out of sight, out of mind?" Never mind that your prospects have your business card, or that they know your number. The onus is on you to build and then maintain "mind share" (that's when your prospect remembers who you are and has kept your name top of mind), and build your customer relationships. Every call you make builds rapport and trust. When you call to keep in touch, you can uncover opportunities, obtain contacts, leads, and referrals, and keep current with changing customer needs.

Over half of my business every year comes from staying in touch with people, existing and former clients, prospects

I've seen, or others I have not. Every few months I place a call to let them know what new challenges I've been asked to remedy. This not only creates an image of my success in their minds (which builds over time), but also opens up a window of opportunity in the event that my prospect happens to be facing a problem similar to the one I'm solving for someone else.

With each and every call I am always generous with sharing ideas and insights, because I know that each time my clients learn something new and useful I am adding value to the customer relationship. Value provides the traction that builds long-term business relationships.

At the end of each conversation I ask the person I am calling when would be the best time to call back to keep in touch. By obtaining permission, I have been given the signal to keep the relationship moving forward. By doing this on a regular basis I make my relationships stronger and keep my finger on the pulse of where and when opportunities will arise.

When opportunity knocks, you too will be standing at the door, ready for when it opens. By applying the techniques you've learned, you'll be creating your own opportunities. Hot Calls open doors and keep them open.

This system also helps you once you're in the door. Leverage the Pot of Gold technique before your meeting. Use your opening line to set the agenda. Apply the same delivery techniques and objection handling skills. If your face-to-face encounter does not culminate in going to the next step, ask yourself, "Is it them or is it me?" and fix the problem before you go out on another sales call. Once you have had a successful meeting and you are scheduling follow-up meetings and calls, use the same Call Planning skills to keep the momentum going. On an ongoing basis, use the power of words to write compelling covering letters and proposals.

The easiest way to build on what you have mastered in Hot Calls is to apply the system found between the pages of my popular sequel, *So Your Foot's In The Door...Now What?* Once you have successfully made the initial customer connection, the sequel will show you how to stay connected until the deal is done. It will keep you in control by showing you how to use islands of structure. Since your conversations are likely to get more involved as your sales cycle progresses, *Foot's In The Door* provides you with a process for creating and testing the content of both your informal and formal presentations.

Now that you have learned how to use this Hot Calls system to successfully generate opportunities, I'd like to share with you the ultimate way to leverage all your good work. I call it a Goal Attainment Strategy. Once you have established a benchmark using this system, you can plan exactly how many calls you will need to make, and how often, in order to reach your goal with one hundred percent certainty. Say for example that under this system you can now book ten appointments out of every fifteen calls. Let's suppose that your close rate (ability to obtain signed contracts) is one sale out of every two face-to-face sales calls. Your goal is ten new sales in one month.

Here's the Goal Attainment Strategy. You'll need twenty appointments to generate ten sales. That means you'll need to make thirty telephone sales calls to generate twenty appointments. Over a one-month period you can now plan on making as little as seven to eight appointments per week. Since your benchmark is based on a system, your goal is assured because you can duplicate your results with one hundred percent certainty. Actually, by constantly self-assessing, you will raise your benchmark and either reach your goal ahead of schedule, or overachieve on the goal with more sales than planned.

Next, reward your milestones, since goals are nothing more than the attainment of milestones. Your Personal Incentive Plan moves from activity-based rewards to goal-based rewards. Key milestones to reward are 50, 80, 100, and 102 percent (if you don't reward overachievement it tends not to happen). Naturally, the higher your bench-mark, the fewer calls you will need to make to reach your goals. Keep up with the self-assessment to get your benchmark as high as possible so that you can realize big productivity gains. Remember, this system is not about making lots of calls, it's about making successful calls. It's all about precision.

So right now I'd like to challenge you to set a goal, make it happen, and reap the rewards.

Thanks for giving me the opportunity to be a part of your success.

Don't Miss Your Calling!

Start Your Hot Cold Calls

by visiting

www.hotcoldcalls.com

- Access FREE powerful Hot Calls self-assessment tools
- Contact Steven J. Schwartz
- Order the popular *How to Make Hot Cold Calls* CD
- Find corporate and personal training programs, seminars, and speeches
- Submit your personal Hot Calls success stories